Youth-Led MEETINGS

VOLUME 1

10 step-by-step meeting plans designed for teenagers to lead themselves

By Dr. Elaine Clanton Harpine

Group Books

Loveland, Colorado

Acknowledgments

I wish to say thank you first to my loving husband, Bill. Without your help, I would never have been able to start or finish the book. Thanks for believing in me.

I am also very grateful to my three wonderful children, David, Virginia and Christina. Thank you for your own special help and hours of patience. And, finally, I wish to express my gratitude to all the young people with whom I've developed youth group meetings over the years. Thank you for the wonderful hours we spent together.

Youth-Led Meetings, Volume 1

Copyright © 1989 by Elaine Clanton Harpine

First Printing

Credits
Edited by Eugene C. Roehlkepartain
Designed by Judy Bienick

Scripture quotations are from The Holy Bible, New International Version. Copyright © 1973, 1978, 1984 International Bible Society. Used by permission of Zondervan Bible Publishers.

ISBN 0-931529-53-0
Printed in the United States of America

Contents

How to Use This Book

I first introduced youth-led meetings to a youth group at a planning retreat. The church had a small but active senior high group and no junior high group. Although only eight group members attended the retreat, they worked hard to plan meetings, projects and activities for the coming year. Once they were finished, they could hardly wait to get started.

During that retreat and the following year, the teenagers grew closer as a group, and they took pride in their work. They had become truly involved in the youth group. Now it was *their* group.

This book is a practical tool for youth-led youth group meetings. It includes the following elements:

● an introductory chapter which presents the rationale and guidelines for youth-led meetings. If you don't already have youth-led meetings, it offers step-by-step ideas for introducing the idea to your church;

● a complete, ready-to-use weekend planning retreat your group can use to plan a complete year of youth group meetings; and

● 10 easy-to-use meetings that your youth group members can lead.

A Simple Approach

It's important to introduce youth-led meetings into a structure that's also youth-led. If your youth group doesn't have an active youth council or other youth leadership group, begin by developing that structure. Chapter 1 offers some suggestions. Another useful tool is *Involving Youth in Youth Ministry* by Thom Schultz and Joani Schultz (Group Books).

Once your leadership group is in place, your next step is to hold a planning retreat to organize a year of meetings, select a youth coordinator for each meeting and begin training group members for leadership. Chapter 2 is a ready-to-use retreat designed specifically to accomplish these goals.

Then it's time to let group members lead each meeting. Here's what to do:

1. Help the meeting coordinator choose a meeting from this book. The introductions to the meetings discuss the meeting content and the coordinators' responsibilities.

2. Work with the coordinator to find different group members to lead each part of the meeting. For example, you may need different leaders for the community-builder, the learning time, the Bible study, the affirmation and so forth. By recruiting several people to help with a meeting, you not only spread around the work, but you give more group members leadership opportunities.

3. Have the meeting coordinator photocopy the instructions for each meeting element to give to each leader. These instructions include: "What You'll Need," "How to Prepare" and "How to Lead." Group members each will need to photocopy the handouts for their part in the meeting.

4. The week before the meeting, touch base with the meeting coordinator and individual leaders as needed. In some cases, the leaders may need extra help from an adult. For example, you may need to help contact hunger organizations for Meeting 3 or find suicide prevention resources for Meeting 9.

An Invitation

Youth-led meetings can help transform an apathetic group of teenagers into an excited youth group. Group members will delight each week in the creative activities they participate in during youth group meetings. They'll blossom as they have the opportunity to lead their peers. And they'll learn the important truth that Christian growth can be fun, exciting and spiritually enriching. Through this book, I invite you and your group to join this exciting and enriching experience.

PART ONE:

Introducing Youth-Led Meetings

Letting Young People Take Charge

CHAPTER 1

6:00 p.m.—*Gail, 15, starts the meeting. She asks the group to gather around a table covered with kitchen utensils. Then she encourages group members to pick utensils that describe themselves as friends. Gail begins the discussion by saying she's most like a sifter because she is picky about the people she spends time with.*

6:10 p.m.—*Marty, 16, brings his guitar to the circle, while Carol, 18, passes out songbooks. Group members call out their favorite songs as the group sings songs about friendship. Sam, 13, announces that tonight's refreshments are friendship fortune cookies. Group members read their "friendship fortunes" to the group.*

6:20 p.m.—*Judy, 14, calls group members to the tables and has them form groups of five to play "The Friendship Maze" board game. Conversation and laughter fill the room as the young people play.*

6:40 p.m.—*As others put away the games, Mike, 17, rearranges group members into seven teams for the Bible study. Mike gives each team its collage supplies and two paper sacks with a Bible verse inside the sacks. Each team makes paper-sack collage blocks that explain its Bible verse.*

6:55 p.m.—*After a discussion about the blocks, Paul, 14, distributes strips of paper. He asks group members each to write a positive comment about each person as that person's paper is passed around the circle. Group members then fold their papers into friendship rings to wear for the rest of the evening.*

7:00 p.m.—*Jackie, 15, has group members form a circle. She passes a ball of string around the circle to symbolize unity. She talks about friendship. Then she passes a pair of scissors around the circle for her friends to cut the string between them to symbolize each person's uniqueness. She has each person tie his or her string through a buttonhole or belt loop as a reminder of how special a friendship can be. Jackie closes the meeting with everyone singing the group's favorite version of the Lord's Prayer.*

Gail, Marty, Carol, Sam, Judy, Mike, Paul and Jackie are not adult leaders. They're regular teenagers who've taken responsibility for leading their church's youth group meetings.

Because they've taken responsibility for planning and leading their own meetings, these young people feel important in their group. As a result, group members attend more regularly, invite more friends and enjoy the activities more.

Benefits of Youth-Led Meetings

Leading their own meetings is a wonderful challenge for the group members, and they feel great pride in their successes. Like everybody else, teenagers work harder when they have responsibility. Giving group members leadership in youth group meetings has many benefits for youth ministry.

Involvement. The first benefit when group members lead their own meetings is involvement. They all participate. Instead of just listening or being told what to do, they make decisions, ask other group members to help them with projects and activities, and lead their peers in activities and study. No one remains a bystander when everyone's a leader.

In one church where I worked, a drama group started because a few young people wanted it. All of them were shy, and only one had any experience. But they wanted to do it. So they formed their drama group and began practicing when the youth choir met (which they weren't involved with).

The drama group became a close-knit, active fellowship. Eventually, the young people even wrote plays and presented them to the church at Christmas and Easter. Their enthusiasm and involvement more than compensated for any lack of skill they might have had. Most important, however, they were significantly involved in the church—involvement that was only possible because they were part of a youth-led group.

Caring. Many young people join youth groups almost begging for acceptance and someone to be their friend. Unfortunately, many young people who desperately need friends have no idea how to make friends.

Michael (not his real name) belonged to a youth group I worked with. He came from a broken home, and he had trouble making friends. But, Michael began coming to youth-led meetings. Before long, he was helping set up for meetings and cleaning up afterward. Because Michael showed up and was available, other group members who needed assistance would ask him to help. Eventually Michael became an active group member. That never would have happened if young people weren't leading the meetings, since they never would have had reason to reach out to him.

When group members plan and lead all aspects of their program, they learn how to share and show they care for one another—probably one of our most important Christian lessons. Being leaders helps young people realize it's their job to make others feel welcome. They can't rely on adults anymore.

Ownership. We're all more inclined to take care of the things we own. If group members feel that the group is truly their own youth group, they'll try harder than ever to make it the best it can be. A feeling of ownership comes when young people feel their efforts make a difference. They simply don't get a full sense of ownership when an adult leads the meetings.

Variety. Another important benefit of youth-led programming is that group members plan a wide variety of activities they enjoy. Adult leaders don't have to guess what teenagers want to do or study; the young people themselves plan what they want.

Group members naturally plan meetings that interest them—problems they're struggling with at home, ideas they hear about at school, questions they have about their faith. And they each bring their own perspective and ideas into a program. The different approaches and emphases provide a rich programming balance.

If I had been planning the meetings, I would never have chosen to have a Career Month. The kids would say, "boooorrring!" Right? Not really. A "Career Month" is exactly what a group planned on an annual retreat. The result: a useful, interesting and successful emphasis.

The same group wanted to do an in-depth study of other religions, including visits to a synagogue and a mosque. I would never have suggested it. It would never work. But the young people wanted it. So we did it. And the experience resulted in a rich, eye-opening educational adventure for the whole group.

Learning. Everyone learns through experiences. Youth-led meetings give teenagers a safe and positive place to learn how to make decisions, be responsible group members and be leaders among their peers. We all need this training for life. And the church can be one of the best places around to learn how to live the Christian life.

Asking group members to lead their own meetings is a terrific way to teach decision-making and leadership skills. By leading meetings, they learn how to respond when things don't go exactly as planned. What do you do when you plan a picnic and it rains? Teenage leaders learn versatility and flexibility.

Leaders also learn that their actions have consequences. If a leader fails to prepare adequately for part of a meeting, the activity probably won't work. On the other hand, they discover that a well-planned meeting can be a powerful growing experience for their peers. As a result, leaders learn to work hard on their commitments to bring about the best possible consequences.

Continuity. Youth-led meetings don't depend on a charismatic youth minister, a great adult leader or a single fantastic group member. Everyone knows about churches where the entire youth program falls apart when a dynamic youth minister leaves. That's because one person planned, organized and led everything. In contrast, a well-organized youth-led program continues year after year with everyone's support—adult leaders, parents, the youth group, the church. Youth-led meetings help you build an effective program for today *and* tomorrow.

The Challenges of Youth-Led Meetings

If youth-led meetings come with so many advantages, why don't more churches implement them? The most obvious reason is tradition: "We've never done it this way before." But there are other reasons too. It's not easy to switch from adult-led to youth-led meetings. Here's why:

Time. Youth-led meetings take more time to plan. It's often quicker to have an adult do all the work. It takes longer to teach someone else how to do something than it takes just to do it yourself.

In order for youth-led meetings to be effective, they require more planning. Group members have to be recruited for different responsibilities. Adult leaders need to help group members gather resources and ideas for the program. And then adults need to check with young people before the meeting to be sure everything is ready.

Adults have to share the spotlight. One of the most challenging jobs for adult workers is to help group members learn and lead without the adults themselves taking credit for successful programs.

I once worked with a youth group where the youth minister enthusiastically believed in youth-led ministry. We held planning retreats at which the group members chose their programs and projects. They brainstormed ideas and planned every detail of their activity calendar. Every group member had a turn to lead.

Then a new minister came. He wanted to be in charge and decide every detail. The youth council was discontinued. Weekend planning retreats—which had become a spiritually enriching tradition—ended. The group's closeness dissipated. And group members stopped coming to meetings. The youth group and its sponsors tried to explain to the newcomer what he was destroying. But his ego prevailed. He saw youth-led ministry as a threat to his authority. He wanted to take over.

Another youth group decided to start youth-led meetings, but adult leaders had trouble getting many group members to attend the planning retreat. So the adults decided to cancel the retreat and plan the programs a month at a time. And they didn't think they really needed to have teenage coordinators for meetings or even youth representatives on the youth council. The result? The same adults ran things as usual. Adult leaders continued to lead meetings, using what they thought met the young people's needs.

The program failed. Group members didn't like the new approach, and adults blamed the problem on the new "youth-led" format. But the program wasn't really youth-led. Unless it is truly and completely planned and led by teenagers, a "youth-led meeting" is not really youth-led.

Everyone must be on the team for youth-led meetings to work. Youth-led meetings are group centered, and there's no room for adults or teenagers to flex their egos.

Adult leaders need to work behind the scenes, giving young people credit for a program's success. We can remind group members of details, and help them figure out ways to solve problems. We can work together with them as a team, supporting and encouraging them in their efforts. And we can celebrate together for jobs well done. As adult sponsors, we can watch proudly as group members lead. Then we can be first in line to congratulate them for their work.

Mistakes. People make more mistakes when they're learning. As a result, some adults are reluctant to let teenagers lead meetings. But such protection does more harm than good. You can't avoid all mistakes, but you can learn from them.

I worked with some young people who planned a meeting on understanding rock music. The leaders decided it would be best to have the meeting at the church and ask someone to bring a stereo. A group member was willing, so everything seemed to be set.

No one anticipated what would happen. When it came time to listen to songs, the stereo owner insisted on being the disc jockey. He wouldn't play songs other people wanted, and he wouldn't listen to the meeting leader. It became an awkward problem that detracted from the meeting content.

After the meeting during our evaluation time, group members discussed the problem and what they had learned from it. They decided it would've been better to meet in someone's home. They would've saved set-up time because a stereo would be all ready. And, since the stereo would probably belong to the parents, they'd avoid some of the possessiveness they encountered. The group also learned the importance of making sure group members each understood their part in a meeting beforehand.

Lessons learned the hard way are rarely forgotten. An adult worker can help group members look over their plans and learn to think ahead to the consequences of their actions and decisions. After all, is there any more important lesson to learn in life?

Lack of experience. Group members who don't have much experience leading groups may not lead meetings with the seasoned pizazz of a youth ministry veteran. Group members may not speak loud enough for everyone to hear them clearly. They may not know how to react when a problem occurs. They may not be able to answer a particular question.

Once a group was having a meeting on friendship. Because of the group's trust level, Amanda (not her real name) felt comfortable asking about homosexuality. She had a longtime friend who was extremely close, and people were teasing Amanda about being a homosexual. What should she do?

The group was silent. No one knew how to respond. After a long silence, I finally pulled my thoughts together and intervened briefly, knowing the topic's sensitivity. I said: "That's a good question, and we don't always think about it." My brief intervention based on my previous leadership experience gave the youth leader enough direction to continue the discussion.

Because most group members don't have much leadership experience, they need adult leaders' support and training. Include training exercises in your annual planning retreats, and offer regular training through the year as needed. Before a group member leads a meeting, touch base with the young person to make sure everything is in order and answer any questions.

Another good practice is to have young people grow gradually into leadership roles. If you have shy group members, start them in background or non-threatening leadership roles. As they develop experience and confidence, they can move into leading discussions and meetings that deal with sensitive issues.

It's also important to keep priorities in mind. Which is more important: to have polished, flawless meetings (which would be led by adults) or to help group members grow in their skills and respect for each other—even if the meetings have a few snags?

Is It Right for Your Group?

You know the benefits of youth-led meetings. And you know the challenges. So is this approach right for *your group*? And if it is, how do you get started?

Youth-led meetings don't happen magically. You can't just announce that you're changing your meeting format next week, and you'd like someone to volunteer to lead the meeting.

Your youth group needs to follow several steps in order to open the doors to successful youth-led meetings.

Three primary factors will shape your meeting and planning process: group members' age, group size and support for the idea.

Group members' age. There's no question that senior-high-age group members can lead youth meetings. Most have the maturity to cope with decisions or problems, and they have the confidence and organizational skills to plan and present a program. Most can lead discussions, prayers, songs, games and activities with only behind-the-scenes support from adults. And while they may need an adult's help in evaluating options and considering consequences, they're completely capable of supplying the ideas and doing the work.

In addition to high schoolers, though, I've also found that junior highers can successfully plan their own meetings. They may not be quite as comfortable leading meetings, and they may need more direction and guidance. But the results are extremely rewarding.

I introduced youth-led ministry techniques to a junior high group that had disbanded. We started the new year with a kick-off activity and weekend planning retreat. During the retreat we developed an events calendar. Then, before each meeting, leaders helped prepare. Group members made telephone calls and helped with the program. Though their meetings were less polished than those led by senior highers, the junior highers took prideful ownership of their planning and leadership.

Group size. In order to have youth-led meetings, you need at least one or two committed group members who can take responsibility for planning and leading. It's nice to have more, but you can do it with just a few. A small number of committed group members *can* plan and conduct youth-led meetings.

So don't be afraid to start with a small group. If you have one interested group member, you have the makings for a fantastic youth group. Remember, Jesus said that as long as two or three people are present, he will be there also (Matthew 18:20).

If just one teenager comes each week, or if just five young people in your group sign up for the planning retreat, start with what you have. Let these group members plan the programs. Once others see the opportunity to lead and share together, they'll join in.

Support. Unless you have support in the youth group among adult leaders and from the church, your efforts to implement youth-led meetings will be frustrating and fruitless.

If you feel alone in your endeavor, here are several ways to build support for youth-led meetings in your church:

1. Include many people in the planning process—group members, parents, youth council members, church leaders. People need to feel that it's "our" program. Unless people claim ownership, they won't support the program for long.

2. Take interest surveys in the youth group. Find out whether the group members are ready and willing to help with planning and leading.

3. Talk with youth council members, adult volunteers and others who are influential in the youth group. Build their interest in the plan, and answer any questions they have.

4. Once you've established a solid base of support, begin publicizing the new emphasis. During announcement times, explain what's happening and why. Spread the word through the church and youth group newsletters. Build excitement and enthusiasm by focusing on the youth group's possibilities.

Getting Going

When you've built solid support for the transition to youth-led meetings, it's time to start planning. Here are six basic steps to starting youth-led meetings:

Step 1: Organize a youth-led planning group. If your youth program doesn't already have a planning group, you need one. A youth council or similar body that makes decisions, solves problems and emphasizes youth involvement is critical to the youth-led meeting format.

Form a youth council or steering committee that includes teenagers, adult leaders, parents and church staff. Include at least one or two group members from each grade represented in your group. Include both active and inactive members on the council.

Once the group is formed, elect youth coordinators to head up the meetings, a youth secretary to keep notes and a youth publicity coordinator to keep the congregation aware of your plans and programs. Choose an adult leader to work with the youth coordinator as a behind-the-scenes stage director to help keep things organized.

(In their book *Involving Youth in Youth Ministry*, published by Group Books, Thom Schultz and Joani Schultz outline a detailed process for organizing a youth-led youth council.)

Step 2: Hold a planning retreat. Have the youth council organize a weekend planning retreat to plan the entire year's meetings, projects and activities for the weekly meetings. Invite all interested group members to attend. The resulting calendar will tell when the group will meet, who's in charge of each meeting and what the meeting will be about. Use the complete, detailed retreat in Chapter 2.

In order for group members to feel ownership in their program, they need to plan it together as a group. I once talked to a church leader who told me that planning for the youth group was quite easy: just transfer the meetings and events from one annual planning calendar to the next.

It all sounds so easy. But it doesn't work. Youth-led meetings won't work unless the group members can choose their own topics and activities. Then you'll have meetings to which group members will want to commit themselves.

Some adults might worry that the group won't want to do any "heavy" topics. That's usually not a problem. In fact, when group members plan, they most often choose tougher topics than adults do! One youth leader was surprised when—without any adult prompting—the group members insisted that the top issue they wanted to discuss in youth group was suicide.

Step 3: Gather good program materials. Without quality resources, teenage leaders will become frustrated in their efforts to plan interesting and effective meetings. People with lots of programming experience may be able to develop ideas from scratch. But most group members need a format to follow.

For example, you might find a magazine article that you and the youth group think really sounds interesting. But unless it has specific meeting ideas, your teenage leaders may have difficulty creating a whole meeting from it. The best resources are youth meeting and idea books with detailed, easy-to-follow instructions. The complete meetings in Part 2 of this book are designed specifically for group members to plan and lead.

When developing programming ideas, your experience and background as an adult leader become invaluable to the youth-led program. Suggest ideas and resources (magazines, books and films or videos). When doing so, use finesse. Don't bulldoze your ideas over the group members, but offer suggestions. "Have you thought about . . ." or "There's an idea you might want to consider . . ." give group members guidance without demanding that they do it "your way."

To help group members have successful youth-led meetings, give them action-oriented meeting outlines to choose from. Strong meetings include activities and learning experiences that involve all participants—small-group experiences, projects, friendly competition. Look for meetings that include:

1. A preparation section that tells the youth leader what supplies to gather and how to prepare for the meeting.

2. At least two or three educational activities that relate to the topic. These might include board games, communication exercises and small group activities. Use meeting elements that stress action and experiences more than discussion. Handout 1-1, "Basic Meeting Ingredients," describes the basic elements for a well-rounded youth group meeting.

3. Step-by-step directions telling the leader exactly how to prepare and conduct the meeting, including specific questions group leaders can use to start discussions.

In many cases you won't find all these qualities in a single source. You might combine two or three ideas from different meetings to get enough material for a solid one-hour meeting. As long as you can tie all the activities to the meeting's theme, it's fine.

You may have to write step-by-step instructions yourself. Meeting suggestions in some books and magazines are only outlines. While these may be adequate guidance for an experienced adult, group members may need more specific instructions that cover all the details— supplies, step-by-step instructions, discussion-starter questions and so forth.

Step 4: Organizing weekly meetings. After you've successfully planned your group's year-long calendar at the retreat, you're ready to put the leaders to work organizing their specific programs. The first week after the retreat, type (or have a group member type) and distribute the calendar to leaders.

Meet with the meeting coordinators listed on the planning calendar from the retreat. Discuss the basic elements of a good meeting: community-builder, learning time, affirmation and closing. Talk about the coordinators' meeting topic, and share ideas and resources with them.

Lead the coordinators through the following steps:

● Select meeting ideas based on the needs and interests you discovered during your retreat. Then select specific activities to use, such as visiting a nursing home or inviting a guest speaker. Have coordinators list their ideas on the planning calendar, to avoid duplication.

● Once they've each selected their meeting and its parts, the coordinators should choose group members (or ask for volunteers) to help lead each part of the meeting. For example, the coordinator may lead the community-builder and ask friends to lead a learning time, a Bible study, an affirmation time and a closing. The meeting coordinators also need to recruit people to help with food and music.

● Encourage the coordinators to check with you if they have questions or have trouble making the meeting pieces fit together.

Step 5: Recruiting leaders. Meeting coordinators should never lead whole meetings themselves. Encourage them to recruit other group members to help them. Learning to delegate and share leadership is an important life skill for the future. How many adults do you know who burn themselves out in volunteer church work because they haven't learned to share the load?

Furthermore, all group members should have an opportunity to lead part of a meeting at least once during the year. If your group is large, you may only have time for group members to lead a program once or twice. On the other hand, small groups can include group members in some sort of leadership several times each month.

If some group members are particularly shy, they might be more willing to "lead" in a background role. This might involve working on refreshments or helping a friend prepare program materials. Then, when they build up con-

Basic Meeting Ingredients

Stir together these seven basic ingredients to cook up a great youth group meeting. They can be arranged in whatever order best fits the meeting theme. And several elements may be combined into one activity. For example, using music during a game can be a great community-builder.

1. Community-builders. Community-builders are fun, structured games, activities and discussion-starters that get group members to interact with each other. Activities should build group unity, boost participants' self-esteem, and provide for appropriate physical contact.

2. Music. Using music in group meetings builds group unity, provides a focus, sets the mood and uses group members' talents. You don't have to be an expert to lead music. Enlist an accompanist from the group or use sing-along tapes. The idea is to have fun together and add to the learning experience through the song's message.

3. Learning time. This is the meeting's central focus. It may include a Bible study, discussion groups, speakers, films, games or anything else that helps group members grow in their faith. The learning part should be relational (involving interaction among group members), wholistic (dealing with people's real-life concerns) and experiential (letting group members learn by doing).

4. Food. Eating together can create oneness, community and sharing. Besides, everyone *likes* to eat. Be creative with the food by symbolically incorporating it into the meeting whenever you can.

5. Affirmation. Group members are bombarded by put-downs daily at school, in sports and in the media. The youth group can counter the negative feelings that result from put-downs by promoting God's idea that people are a precious creation. Make sure group members give and receive positive reinforcement. Positive words and actions can be simple or creative. In either case, they'll be powerful.

6. Prayer. Prayer is a central ingredient in connecting ourselves to God. Avoid stuffy, wordy or cliché prayers. Speak to God naturally—just as you'd speak to a good friend. You can pray in different ways too, involving the whole group in communication with God.

7. Closing. The meeting's end is as important as a good first impression. It wraps the meeting up into a memorable package. Your youth group can develop its own closing ritual, or you can vary the closing from week to week, depending on the program topic.

fidence, they can assume more responsibility. And because each meeting has several sections, some group members may choose to work on one section as a team.

Another good way to help group members overcome their self-consciousness is to offer them leadership training. A planning retreat or special workshops provide an ideal, non-threatening setting for learning leadership techniques, practicing skills and developing meetings. While not extensive, such training gives group members the self-confidence to lead a meeting.

An excellent training resource is *Developing Youth as Leaders* (Group Publishing), which is a video training tool for youth groups. It covers such topics as "Christlike Leadership," "Listening and Communication," "Decision-Making," "Sharing Leadership," "Group Dynamics" and "Growing Through Failure."

Step 6: Preparation. It's critical that an experienced adult work with each teenage leader to develop ideas, find good resources and plan carefully in order to help leaders come to meetings fully prepared. You can facilitate this preparation through phone calls, notes and other reminders to leaders. Meeting preparation checklists (like those used in Part 2 of this book) are excellent tools for making sure leaders cover all the bases for a particular meeting. Handout 1-2, "Leadership Tips," includes basic leadership guidelines you can photocopy and give to meeting leaders.

The Adult Leader's Role

With group members leading the meetings, where do adult leaders fit in? It's important to emphasize that adults play just as critical a role in youth-led meetings as they do when they lead meetings themselves. The difference is that adults are backstage prompters and supporters, not actors on center stage.

The most important time for the adult leader is *before* the meeting, making sure the meeting leaders are ready. Someone who's prepared ahead of time will be more likely to relax and have fun leading the meeting. Let's look at ways adults can help:

Have a well-planned calendar. The adult leader needs to help young people learn how to plan and organize as a group. By helping leaders organize behind the scenes, you give them

confidence and security when they're leading because they've already worked with you to iron out any wrinkles in their activity. Touch base with leaders before a meeting to see if they have questions or need help. Prepare an agenda for each meeting so leaders will each know when it's time for their part of the meeting.

Adults also play a role in reminding leaders when to organize and how much organizing to do before a meeting. The adult leader's role is to remind, ask questions, help with logistics and prompt the young people as they plan.

Help anticipate problems. As an adult, you have a responsibility and opportunity to share your wisdom during the planning process. Help meeting planners think through possible problems, dangers and consequences of meetings they plan. If the leaders plan an outdoor activity for a meeting, do they have contingency plans in case of bad weather? Have they taken precautions to ensure safety? Are they aware of the potential problems and issues that could arise in discussing a particularly sensitive subject? These kinds of questions are important for adults to ask before the meeting.

Andrew (not his real name) was a member of one youth group I worked with. He was impossible to deal with—and everyone knew it. He'd sit in the last row during meetings. He'd prop his chair against the wall, roll his eyes and make occasional snide remarks. And he never cooperated or participated in the meeting.

Because I knew Andrew would always be at the meeting, I would ask leaders how they planned to handle him. Some chose to ignore him. Others tried (to no avail) to include him. Whatever they decided, though, it always helped that they had addressed the issue beforehand so that they weren't caught off guard by his first sarcastic remark.

Provide support during meetings. To this point, we've talked about the adult leader's role before meetings. But what about during the meeting? How can adults help during a meeting without interfering? The adult's job during the meeting is to be available to answer questions, help when asked, keep track of time, offer a suggestion if someone has trouble, and give reassuring nods or subtle cues. If the leaders have planned well, the adults may not need to do much of anything—just sit back and enjoy a great meeting!

Guide evaluation after meetings. Finally, adult leaders fill an important role by helping the teenage leaders evaluate the meetings. Help them talk about what worked and what didn't. Talk about feelings, fears, discoveries, satisfaction. This debriefing helps leaders learn from their experience. They can discuss what to do if a similar situation arises later.

Meeting the Challenge

Implementing youth-led meetings is a challenge! But it's also a wonderful opportunity for young people to learn and grow in their Christian faith. With training and experience, they can successfully lead their own group meetings. As an adult, you have the privilege of watching them stretch themselves, learn new skills and become leaders in the youth group and church today and in the future.

Enjoy the challenge. Laugh about the foibles. Cheer the successes. And celebrate the spiritual growth you see in your youth group and its new leaders. The satisfaction you find in the new approach will be well worth the effort.

Leadership Tips

If you're a little unsure about leading your youth group meeting, relax. There are a few easy things you can do to make sure everything goes smoothly.

Preparation

● Begin preparing well in advance—at least two or three weeks, depending on the meeting.

● Carefully read the instructions for leading the activity. Be sure you understand how the activity works, what you need to do and what supplies you need. If you have questions, check with your meeting coordinator or your adult helper.

● Gather all the supplies you'll need for the meeting. Check with your adult helper before spending any money on supplies or resources. Keep all the materials together for the meeting.

● Do any necessary preparation well in advance of the meeting (making game boards, preparing and photocopying handouts, selecting music and so forth). Don't put it off until the last minute; you may run out of time.

● Arrive for the meeting early. This gives you a chance to relax, and it lets group members know that you're excited about the meeting.

Leading Discussions

● Before the meeting, prepare questions that you can ask to get the discussion going.

● Avoid questions with yes or no answers. For example, instead of asking, "Do you like the song?" you could ask, "What do you like or dislike about the song?"

● Include many people in the discussion. If one or two group members are answering all your questions, ask others by name—particularly if you think they might have a good perspective: "Maria, what do you think Jesus meant in this verse?" "Jon, as a football player, how do you view what this verse says about competition?"

● Don't dominate the discussion yourself. Since you've spent more time studying the issue you're discussing, you may have lots of things to say. Avoid the temptation to lecture. Instead, help group members think through the issue themselves.

A Ready-to-Use Planning Retreat

A planning retreat is a key ingredient in a youth-led youth ministry. The retreat format involves young people in intensive planning more effectively than other formats. And by planning a year at once, it's easier to provide balance and variety in your program.

Youth group planning can be fun—not long, boring or frustrating. The following retreat is a fun and effective way to have young people design their youth program for the next year. In doing so, they will take prideful ownership in "our" youth program. The retreat will help your group members:

● express what's important to them;
● strengthen friendships;
● plan a year's worth of youth group meetings based on their interests; and
● learn how to lead youth group meetings.

Getting Ready

The more group members who attend a planning retreat, the better. Broad participation translates into broad leadership. However, you don't have to have a large group to have a successful retreat. I once conducted a planning retreat with only eight teenagers. Those young people worked hard on the retreat and planned a great calendar.

As the year went on, more and more young people heard about the great meetings these group members planned. More started coming to meetings, and I heard many comments about the retreat, like: "I wish I had been there" and "Next year I'm going." When it came time for next year's retreat, we had more than 20 young people who wanted to attend.

Retreat leadership. A successful retreat requires advance planning and publicity. Begin organizing and publicizing the retreat at least three months in advance. Get as many group members as possible to attend the retreat.

Select one or two adults to oversee retreat planning and leadership. However, it's also important to include young people in the retreat planning to set the stage for your youth-led pro-gram. Here are three groups to form to help with specific tasks:

● the youth council or steering committee, to help arrange the retreat;
● a retreat planning committee (of youth and adults), which gathers supplies and makes retreat materials; and
● youth council members to lead the closing worship service.

Date and location. Give the youth council or steering committee responsibility for arranging the retreat's date, location, registration fee and other logistical details. *Fast Forms for Youth Ministry* (Group Books) provides a variety of forms and checklists for retreat planning. The retreat center or camp you select sets the mood for the weekend. Be particular, start early, and ask for what you want from the retreat center's management.

Include on the registration form a list of what to bring, scheduled departure and return times, and some idea of what the group can expect to do during the weekend. Deposits, written medical release forms and parental consent forms reduce the last-minute cancellations.

Publicity. Assign publicity to creative retreat planning committee members. Use as many methods as you can to publicize your retreat. Creative skits or announcements after worship, posters, church newsletter articles, Sunday bulletin inserts, telephone calls and mailings all help promote enthusiasm and interest in the retreat. Start publicity at least three months before the retreat so people can mark it on their calendars.

Gathering materials. The retreat planning committee helps prepare retreat materials. (This is good training for group members to learn how to prepare meeting materials when they lead regular meetings.) Here's what the committee needs to do:

● Gather all the supplies listed in Handout 2-1. Put them in a large box to take to the retreat. Add all the other materials you prepare for the retreat.

• Prepare the "What Matters Most" game cards, theme circle and wall chart (Handouts 2-2 and 2-3 pages 19-20). Make a set of 60 game cards for every 10 players.

• Make a colorful paper banner that says: "Welcome to the Quiz Game."

• Choose a meeting from the back of this book for the Saturday evening training session. Find one that takes few props and little preparation. (Meetings 1, 2 and 4 would be appropriate.) Gather all the materials needed for the meeting.

• Make a rainbow-shape banner out of newsprint for the closing worship service. Across the top of the banner write: "A Rainbow of New Beginnings." Leave space on the banner for the group to create a rainbow.

• Write on newsprint the instructions for "More Than a Name" Tag.

• Make a "Love Your Neighbor" jigsaw puzzle for the Saturday evening celebration by enlarging Handout 2-5, gluing it to cardboard, and cutting out enough irregular-shape puzzle pieces so everyone on the retreat (including adult sponsors) will have one piece.

• Photocopy the following: "Nature Scavenger Hunt List" (Handout 2-4) and "Retreat Evaluation" (Handout 2-6) for all participants.

Suggested Retreat Schedule

Friday

7:00 p.m.	Arrive and unpack
7:30 p.m.	Committing to the Weekend
7:45 p.m.	"More Than a Name" Tag
8:30 p.m.	Free time/Refreshments
8:45 p.m.	Planning Session 1—What Matters Most?
10:00 p.m.	Free time
10:30 p.m.	Evening Celebration—Sharing a Penny
11:30 p.m.	Lights out

Saturday

7:30 a.m.	Morning Call—The Orange Exchange
7:45 a.m.	Breakfast
9:00 a.m.	Planning Session 2—The Quiz Game
10:15 a.m.	Break
10:30 a.m.	Nature Scavenger Hunt
11:30 a.m.	Free time
Noon	Lunch
1:00 p.m.	Planning Session 3—Putting the Pieces Together

Handout 2-1

Materials Checklist

Place the following materials (along with the other items you prepare) in a large box for the retreat.

☐ 4×6 index cards for name tags
☐ 3×5 cards for everyone
☐ Candles and matches
☐ Newsprint
☐ Felt-tip markers in bright, easy-to-read colors
☐ Plenty of paper
☐ Pencils for everyone
☐ Masking tape
☐ Noise makers for each team (such as a jingle bell on a string, a kazoo, a dinner bell or a baby's rattle)
☐ Colorful round stickers (eight per person)—available from office supply stores
☐ Calendars and schedules (from church, schools, clubs, community organizations and other relevant groups)
☐ A Bible for each person
☐ Snack prizes

☐ Scissors for everyone
☐ Fresh oranges (one per person)
☐ Songbooks
☐ Pennies for each group member
☐ An empty pickle jar
☐ A large paper sack for each group of three to five people
☐ Cellophane tape or a stapler
☐ Glue
☐ Sports equipment for group recreation time
☐ Construction paper strips (about 1"×8½")—three per person
☐ Old magazines for making collages
☐ Felt and other banner-making materials
☐ Cardboard
☐ Paper cups

3:30 p.m.	Group Recreation Time
4:30 p.m.	Planning Session 4—Final Touches
5:00 p.m.	Dinner
6:00 p.m.	Free time
6:30 p.m.	Training Session—Preparation
8:30 p.m.	Free time/Refreshments
9:00 p.m.	Training Session—Leading the Meeting
10:00 p.m.	Free time/Refreshments
10:15 p.m.	Evening Celebration—Love Your Neighbor
11:30 p.m.	Lights out (or at other agreed-upon time)

Sunday

7:00 a.m.	Morning Call—In Search of New Beginnings
7:45 a.m.	Breakfast
8:45 a.m.	Worship—New Beginnings
11:30 a.m.	Cleanup and pack
Noon	Lunch
1:00 p.m.	Evaluation
2:30 p.m.	Leave for home

Friday Evening

Plan to arrive at your retreat site in time to unpack, get settled and explore before beginning your evening session. You may choose to arrive in time for dinner. Or eat enroute to the retreat center.

The adult leader facilitates the evening planning sessions, which revolve around games and activities that make planning fun.

Committing to the Weekend

At the front of the room, post a sheet of newsprint labeled "Weekend Contract" for people to sign. As group members gather for the evening program, discuss the retreat's purpose, schedule and rules. Agree as a group to a lights-out time, and answer any questions about the retreat. Have group members agree to the rules and restrictions by having them each sign their name or initials on the sheet of newsprint. Also ask them each to write one thing they'll contribute to the group during the weekend. For example, someone could write, "I'll give creative meeting ideas" or "I'll give my undivided attention to planning."

"More Than a Name" Tag

After everyone has signed the "Weekend Contract" newsprint, give each person (including adults) a 4×6 index card to make a name tag.

Have different-color felt-tip markers for them to use. Post newsprint with these instructions nearby:

● Print your name neatly in the upper right-hand corner. (If everybody already knows everyone well, write your favorite celebrity's name instead of your own name.)

● In the center of the card, draw a picture of the kind of person you are—friendly, moody, indecisive, happy, confused, outgoing, shy, angry and so forth. Don't draw how you look physically; picture how you feel inside. If you're not sure how you feel, then draw a picture depicting that.

● In the lower right-hand corner, write your favorite activity or hobby.

● In the lower left-hand corner, describe your favorite time of day.

● In the upper left-hand corner, write one or two words that say what you like most about your best friend.

● Then on the back of your name tag, write why you came to the retreat and what you expect to do this weekend.

Allow about five minutes for group members to complete their name tags. Use masking tape to attach name tags. Then have group members form pairs. Have partners each introduce themselves to their partner and explain their name tag. Keep the pace brisk. Allow about five minutes.

Next, have each pair join another pair to form a foursome. Have each person introduce his or her partner to the others. Allow about 10 minutes.

When everyone has been introduced in the small group, form a discussion group in a circle of chairs. (Don't sit around tables or in rows; you'll destroy the togetherness you've been developing.) Invite teenagers each to tell something they have in common with someone they've met in their small group. If you have time, ask participants to tell about their pictures.

Then take a 15-minute break for refreshments and informal conversations.

Planning Session 1—What Matters Most?

Before you begin, tape the Theme Wheel (see Handout 2-2) to the wall. Divide the group into teams of 10. (If you have fewer than 10 people, form smaller groups of three or four people, and adjust the directions as needed.) Give

What Matters Most Game

Theme Wheel. Enlarge the following chart to poster size. Print shops can enlarge it for you on card stock, or draw it yourself on poster board.

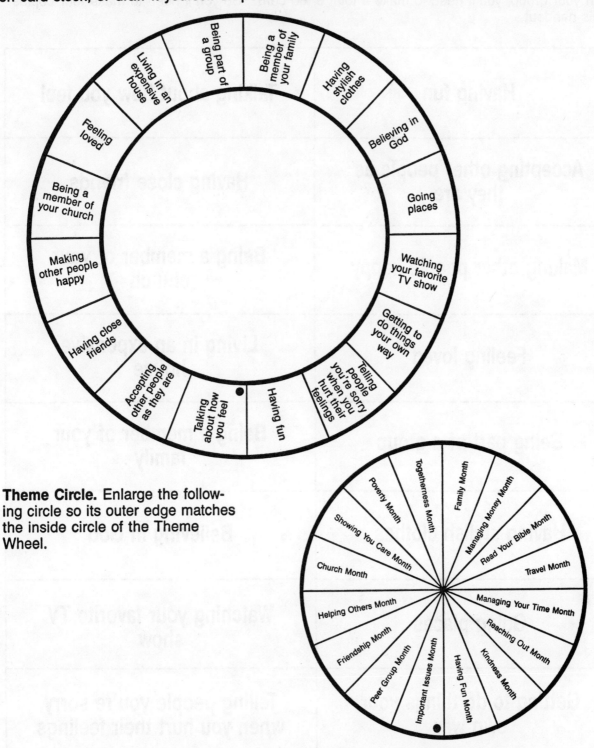

Theme Circle. Enlarge the following circle so its outer edge matches the inside circle of the Theme Wheel.

What Matters Most Game Cards

Photocopy the following boxes; then cut them out and paste them on 3×5 cards. Make enough duplicates for each group member to have six cards. For example, if you have 10 people in your group, you'll need to make a total of 60 cards. So you'll need to make four copies of this handout.

Having fun	**Talking about how you feel**
Accepting other people as they are	**Having close friends**
Making other people happy	**Being a member of your church**
Feeling loved	**Living in an expensive house**
Being part of a group	**Being a member of your family**
Having stylish clothes	**Believing in God**
Going places	**Watching your favorite TV show**
Getting to do things your own way	**Telling people you're sorry when you hurt their feelings**

each group 60 "What Matters Most Game Cards"—six cards for each member. Then explain the game:

"What Matters Most" is a card-trading game that will help us choose our youth group's monthly themes for the next year. We've given each team a set of 60 cards with statements written on them. The object of the game is to end up with the six cards that come closest to describing what matters most to you. Some of the cards are duplicates, so more than one person can end up with a particular card. The Theme Wheel topics match the cards.

To begin the game, shuffle the cards and deal six cards to each player. Look at the Theme Wheel chart and decide which cards you'd like. Then look at your "hand," and set aside any cards you want in your final six. Trade away the cards you don't want.

When everyone's ready, begin trading within your team. Don't tell others exactly which cards you have; only give one-word hints. For example, if you want to trade away the card "Talking about how you feel," you could say, "Sharing." If you really want a particular card, you can offer two cards for it. You may get up and move around as you trade, but stay with your team. Hurry—or someone may get a card you want!

When one player has the six cards he or she wants, that player stops and marks his or her choices on the Theme Wheel chart underneath the appropriate topic. The other players continue trading until all players have at least three cards they want. Then remaining players discard what they don't want and mark their choices on the wheel.

After you've explained the rules and answered questions, tell the teams to begin.

When everyone has marked choices on the wheel, add up the scores for each topic and rank the top 12 from most to least interest. Then place the Theme Circle in the middle of the Theme Wheel so that the two dots line up. This shows how the 12 top choices can become monthly youth group themes. You can then use these as your group's topics, or you may rewrite the themes as needed.

Free Time

After the theme session, take a 30-minute break. During this break, write the top 12 monthly themes on separate sheets of newsprint so you'll be ready to put together the calendar on Saturday afternoon.

Evening Celebration—Sharing a Penny

Light candles and turn off all the lights in the meeting room. Have your pickle jar of pennies for all group members nearby. Call the group back together, and have everyone sit in a circle on the floor. Create a relaxed atmosphere by singing songs or sharing feelings about the evening.

Then tell the following "Sharing a Penny" story:

One day a girl named Casey found a jar while she and her mother were cleaning the hall closet. The jar had a penny in it. She asked her mother what the jar was for.

"I don't know," her mother responded. "Your dad probably put it there and forgot about it. After all, it's just an old pickle jar with a penny in it. Here, take the penny," she said, taking off the lid. "Then throw the jar away."

"Oh, can I have the jar too?" Casey asked.

"Yes, yes, of course," her mother said. "Now, why don't you play out in the back yard while I finish cleaning this closet."

So Casey took her shiny penny and her old pickle jar that still smelled of dill pickles and sat on the back porch.

"I wonder what I could do with these," Casey mumbled, as she rubbed the penny to make it shinier. "I can't buy anything with just a penny. And this pickle jar smells too much to put anything else in it."

As she sat there looking around, she glanced down and noticed another penny lying in the dust by the porch step. It wasn't pretty and shiny like her other penny. It was dirty and dark. And as she examined it more closely, it looked as if someone had tried to cut it in half. But, after all, a penny is a penny, so she dropped it into her pickle jar.

What could she do with two pennies? Not much. But if she looked around some more, maybe, just maybe, she'd find more. So she began her search.

About that time her big brother came bounding into the yard. "What are you doing, Casey?" he inquired.

"Looking for pennies. See, I already have two," she replied.

"Oh, let me see if I have any," Jake said. He poked his fingers down into his pockets and pulled out three quarters. "Nope. No pennies today."

"Oh, that's okay," Casey said, sort of sadly. "Here. Take one of mine. I can't do anything with just two pennies anyway."

Casey wandered off with her pickle jar and her one shiny penny. (At least she gave Jake the old, chewed-up penny.) About that time, her dad pulled up. Casey ran to meet him.

"What do you have, Casey?" her dad asked as he got out of the car.

"Just an old pickle jar with a penny in it," Casey told him.

"Well, let me see if I have any pennies to add to your collection."

Her dad reached into his pocket. "Here you go," he said, pulling out six pennies and placing them in the jar.

"Thanks," Casey said.

Just then Casey's mom came out of the house heading for the grocery store. She asked Casey if she wanted to go. "Sure," Casey said. Anything's better than sitting around the house.

Casey followed her mother through the store, still carrying her pickle jar with seven pennies. Casey was trying to decide whether to buy some gum or to save the pennies and try to collect more. Before she could make up her mind, her mom was at the checkout counter digging in her purse for more money to pay the cashier.

"How much do you need?" Casey asked.

"Oh, just five cents," her mother said.

Casey pulled five pennies out of her jar and gave them to her mother.

"Thank you, Casey," her mother said. "I'll pay you back later."

Casey looked at her jar; there were just two old pennies left. Casey had mistakenly given away all her shiny new ones. Her mother hadn't even asked to borrow Casey's pennies. But then, pennies are pennies, Casey thought. And her mother kept saying how nice it was of Casey to loan her five pennies. Then a man in the next aisle unexpectedly reached over and dropped three pennies into Casey's jar. Casey tried to say thanks, but the man just smiled and pushed his cart out the door.

"Wow! Now I have five pennies!" Casey thought to herself.

The pickle jar sat on the kitchen counter for weeks. One day Jake needed five cents, so Casey gave him her five pennies. Two days later, she saw eight pennies in the jar. "Where did these come from?" she wondered out loud.

"I repaid you with interest," her mother said as she walked by. How interesting! The more pennies Casey gave away, the more she had. People she didn't even know gave her pennies just because she had given pennies to others who needed them.

Then Casey had an idea. "I'm going to try an experiment," she thought. "I'm going to take my pickle jar to school today, and every time

someone needs a penny, I'll give them one of mine."

And so she did. She gave her pennies out one by one until she had only one left. Then she saw Mary, a girl she didn't even like very much, sitting on a playground bench, crying. Casey didn't know what was wrong, but she felt sad.

Then she thought, "When people need money and I give them my pennies, they're happy and grateful. Maybe if I give her a penny, it would cheer up Mary too." So Casey reached into her pickle jar and gave Mary her last penny. Mary took the penny and mumbled, "Thanks."

Casey walked on, but Mary suddenly came running up behind her, still holding the penny. Then she dropped another penny in Casey's jar.

Now Casey always carries a penny with her wherever she goes. And when she sees someone who needs a "hello," a "thank you" or a special "I like you," Casey takes out one of her pennies—shiny and old alike—and gives it away with confidence. She knows that the more she gives the more she'll receive.

After the story, give each group member a penny from your jar. As you circle the group, say: I want to share a penny with each of you. Do as you wish with this penny. Save it to buy something later. Give one to someone as a token of friendship. Give it to someone to say "thanks" for something he or she has done. Or offer it to someone to say, "I'd like to get to know you better." You don't have to share your penny right now. But always remember during this retreat the meaning a little penny can have and how many times a penny can be shared.

Close with a prayer, thanking God for the gifts we have which we can share with each other. Encourage group members to share their pennies throughout the retreat.

Saturday Morning
Morning Call—The Orange Exchange

As group members arrive, give each an orange. Say: Study your orange very carefully. Find something unique about it—one thing that makes it different from everyone else's orange. For example, your orange may have a crease at a particular place, or it may be green in one spot.

Once group members are acquainted with their oranges, have them each describe to a partner their orange's distinguishing feature.

Then have the group members form a circle, each still holding their orange. Tell them to pass their oranges to the right around the circle as fast as they can. After a few seconds, call "stop." Then have group members pass their oranges to the left. Have them toss oranges across the circle to make it even harder. Then go back and forth to the right and left until no one knows where his or her orange is.

Then tell group members to pass the oranges very slowly to their right so they can find the orange they had at the beginning. After a few minutes, ask for a show of hands of those who are sure they have their original orange.

Next, explain that although each orange is different, oranges are also very much the same. And we, just like oranges, share many qualities and yet also have distinguishing characteristics and personalities. Spend a few minutes discussing how group members are the same and how each is different. Ask:

● What distinguishing characteristics identify everyone as a youth group member?

● What are some characteristics we all share together?

● What qualities do you think you have that make you different from others in the group?

Close the discussion by reminding everyone that each person has something to contribute to the group, and that the group has something to give each person: acceptance. Have group members read aloud the following two scripture passages: Matthew 7:12 and Romans 13:8-10. Close with a prayer, thanking God for the many gifts he has given each of us.

Then have the group members take their oranges to breakfast. Give each person a cup. Slice the oranges in half, and have group members each squeeze some orange juice for someone else in the group who they're getting to know better during the retreat. Make sure each person gets a glass of freshly squeezed orange juice.

Planning Session 2—The Quiz Game

After breakfast, lead this brainstorming session for youth group plans. "The Quiz Game," with competition between teams, makes the brainstorming session fun.

Tape a colorful paper banner across the front of the room that says: "Welcome to the Quiz Game." Place a sheet of newsprint labeled "Best Ideas from Round 1" under the banner.

Divide the group into teams of three. Use masking tape to mark off large squares on the floor for each team (about 12 × 12 feet each, if possible). Give each team a pencil, a noise maker and several sheets of paper. Then explain Round 1.

Round 1. Welcome to "The Quiz Game." You are contestants in a fast-paced Quiz Game. Before we begin, make up a name for your team. Write it at the top of your paper. Choose a secretary to write your team's ideas.

I'll ask you 10 questions. After I read each question, your team must quickly decide its answer. Make your ideas good and realistic, since the team with the most points at the end of Round 3 wins. Sound your noise maker as soon as you've written down all five ideas. Your secretary must completely finish writing all five ideas before you sound the noise maker. The first team finished on each question gets to write one idea for that question on the "Best Ideas from Round 1" sheet. So work fast.

When everyone understands Round 1, begin reading the questions slowly. After each question, check that the first team to sound its noise maker has written down all five ideas. Then let its secretary write one idea on the "Best Ideas" sheet. If you have a tie, let both teams write an idea. Do the same for each question. Allow about 15 minutes for this round. Here are the questions:

1. What are five things you enjoy doing together as a group?

2. What are five things we could do as a group to help other people?

3. What are five things we could do to encourage other teenagers to join our group?

4. What are five questions you have about the Bible that you'd like to discuss?

5. What are five fun ways we could raise money as a group?

6. What are five topics you'd like to learn more about?

7. What are five ways we could become a closer group of friends?

8. What are five things you worry about?

9. What are five ways to be a better person?

10. What are five problems group members face every day?

When you've finished all the questions, sound a noise maker and announce the end of

Round 1. Make sure each team has its name on each paper, and collect all the sheets.

Round 2. Ask each team to join another team to form six-person teams for Round 2. Give each team the sheets from two other teams from Round 1. Make sure no team has its own sheet. Also give each team four sheets of newsprint, a felt-tip marker and a noise maker. Then explain Round 2:

In Round 2, you'll decide which ideas from Round 1 you like the most. There are four categories: faith studies, projects, activities and daily living meetings.

First, look over the sheets of ideas you have. Decide which of these ideas you like the most. Then categorize each of them into one of four categories:

1. *Faith studies* are times set aside for studying scripture and faith issues. A meeting can include games and activities that bring the Bible to life. Participants learn something new while sharing with one another. These meetings can focus on world issues you want to know more about from a Christian perspective—conservation, peace, hunger, abortion.

2. *Projects* include both fund-raising and service projects. They might include recycling aluminum cans or raking leaves to raise money for hunger relief efforts.

3. *Activities* are to be fun, group-building occasions such as a trip, a game night at the church or a dinner together.

4. *Daily living meetings* focus on issues we deal with in our everyday lives. Meetings to explore issues such as sexuality, drug abuse, family relationships or school pressure fit into this category.

When your group has chosen all the best ideas, write your favorites in each category on the newsprint. Use a different sheet for each category. The whole group will vote on your ideas in Round 3, so be sure your group can actually do the ideas you nominate.

Allow the teams about 30 minutes to complete their work. Have them turn in their sheets when they're done.

Round 3. Display the four category sheets each group listed in Round 2. Put all the faith study sheets on one wall together, the project sheets on another wall, and so on. Then ring your noise maker and announce: Election time! You've submitted your nominations. Now it's time to vote. Keep Round 3 very fast-paced.

Give each group member eight colorful stickers to use for voting. Each person can vote for only two ideas in each category at a time. Have group members circulate among the idea sheets from Round 2, putting stickers beside their two top choices in each category.

After group members have voted on all four categories, add up the votes for each idea. Mark the top 12 vote-getters in each category. Then count which winning ideas came from each team in Round 1. Announce the winning team, and present the team with a snack prize that group members can share. Use the snack as your refreshments for a break time.

Nature Scavenger Hunt

After the break, divide into small teams of three to five people. Give each team a "Nature Scavenger Hunt List" (Handout 2-4) and a paper sack for collecting. Allow about 45 minutes for teams to find the items. Have a set time for everyone to return. When everyone returns, have each group show what it found. Then save the findings for Sunday's worship service. Break for lunch.

Saturday Afternoon

Planning Session 3—Putting the Pieces Together

If you haven't already done so, write the 12 themes from Planning Session 1 on newsprint—one theme per sheet. Also ask someone to list the 12 winning ideas from each category—faith studies, projects, activities and daily living meetings—on sheets of newsprint (one sheet per category). Post the 12 calendar sheets from Planning Session 1 and the four master category lists from Planning Session 2.

The goal of this session is to complete your 12-month calendar. You'll:

● pick a theme from Planning Session 1's theme sheets for each month;

● select one faith study, project, activity and daily living meeting idea from Planning Session 2's category sheets to go with each monthly theme; and

● list a coordinator for each meeting.

Begin by having the group pick a theme for September. Write dates for each meeting that month, and check school, church and other calendars for conflicts. Then have group mem-

Nature Scavenger Hunt List

Find or make each of the following items:

1. Something simple
2. Something that could be used as a candle holder
3. Something beautiful
4. Something to symbolize love
5. A wild flower
6. Materials to make a bird feeder
7. Five different leaves (not poison ivy!)

8. Make a cross from things you find in the woods
9. A bird feather
10. Something to give to someone as a friendship token
11. Something that makes you feel happy
12. Something to symbolize peace
13. Something new
14. A black rock

bers decide on one faith study, project, activity and daily living meeting idea that fits the month's theme. Write their ideas on the appropriate calendar pages. Choose a coordinator for each meeting, and write his or her name on the sheet. Make sure everyone has a chance to lead.

Follow the same process for every month until you've planned the whole year. Remember months with holidays; your group may want to plan something special that's not on the category sheets.

Group Recreation Time

After the intense work, group members need to release some physical energy. Plan a high-energy group activity such as volleyball, flag football or basketball.

Planning Session 4—Final Touches

Take off all papers from the walls except the 12 calendar pages. Arrange chairs where everyone can see the calendars. When everyone has gathered, go through each month, making sure your schedule is complete. Check to be sure you have the following:

● At least one meeting from each category planned for each month.
● No schedule conflicts with church, school or other activities.
● A coordinator for each meeting.
● Special plans for holidays, if you wish.

When you've finished double-checking, your basic yearly planning is complete. Celebrate with a special dinner. Then allow free time for people to relax and get ready for the evening.

Saturday Evening

Once you've established your calendar for the year, the next step will be to plan the weekly meetings. The meeting coordinator will be responsible for arranging the specific plans through the year—assisted by adult leaders and various young people who help lead meetings.

Since your group members may not have experience leading meetings, use the evening to teach the basic elements of meeting preparation and leadership. This exercise will give the group members experience and encouragement in preparing for meetings, leading a meeting and handling problems that arise.

Training Session—Preparation

Divide the group into enough teams so that each team can lead one part of the meeting you chose. For example, if the meeting has a community-builder, a learning time, a Bible study, an affirmation and a closing, you'll need five teams. Have each team prepare and lead one section of the meeting. (If you choose, the participants could plan to lead the same meeting for the whole youth group when you go home, if a large portion of your youth group isn't at the retreat.)

Follow the same steps you'd use in preparing for and leading a meeting (except that a whole team will do what one person might normally do). When all the teams have prepared their parts, have a free time with refreshments.

Training Session—Leading the Meeting

Reconvene and have each team lead its section of the meeting for the rest of the group. If you wish, have different group members pretend to be "problem people" during the meeting. For example, two group members could whisper and pass notes in the back row. Someone else could refuse to cooperate with activities. Have each team work together to deal with the problem.

Between meeting sections, stop the meeting and lead the group through an evaluation. Have leaders mention the problems they encountered and the questions they have. Have group members offer affirmation and suggestions.

Emphasize the importance of being positive. Give examples of how easy it is to make a positive gesture toward other group members. For example, you could commend a group member's leadership by saying: "Paul, I really liked the way you included all group members in the discussion." Or, "You do a great job of asking follow-up questions, Annette. I liked the way you included John and Mary in the discussion instead of dominating it yourself." You set a good example by being positive in your evaluations.

Talk about what went well during the training meeting, and give examples of how the leaders involved everyone in the group. Stress ways the leaders helped group members feel at ease and comfortable. Give helpful suggestions, but don't criticize.

It's important now to build confidence within the safe environment of the planning retreat. Remind young people that they're all learning together, so no one is expected to do a "perfect" job. Affirm each person after he or she helps lead.

Thank members for all their hard work and planning. Take a break after the training sessions and offer free time and refreshments before the evening celebration.

Evening Celebration—Love Your Neighbor

As group members gather for the evening celebration, give them each a piece of the "Love Your Neighbor Puzzle" (Handout 2-5) and three strips of colorful construction paper (about 1″×8½″). Make sure they all have their Bibles and pennies from the Friday night story as well. Have cellophane tape or a stapler available to fasten the chain.

Form a circle with everyone sitting on the floor. Begin with group singing to help group members relax. Then put your puzzle piece in the center of the circle, and ask group members and adult sponsors to fit their puzzle pieces with yours.

When the puzzle is done, read aloud Matthew 22:36-39 from the puzzle. Ask:
● What did Jesus mean by "neighbor"?
● Do neighbors include members of our youth group?
● What can we do to help each other?

Then ask group members to write the following on their three strips of paper: On one strip, group members each write their own name. On another strip, they each write the name of someone they've become better friends with during the retreat. On the third strip, group members each write the name of someone in the group they'd like to get to know better.

Next, have group members tape their strips together to make a chain. Then have them fasten their chains to their neighbor's to create a complete circle. Invite group members each to share a favorite Bible verse, song, prayer or thought. Then sing a song and share pennies. Close with a prayer.

Sunday Morning

This final morning helps build enthusiasm in your group for the new direction you've set for the coming year. These Sunday morning activities provide inspiration for the future, and they remind the teenagers of who gives them direction.

Morning Call—In Search of New Beginnings.

As group members gather, have them join hands in one long line. Ask them to join hands with at least one person they haven't had a chance to work with in a small group during the retreat. Then say that they're going on a nature walk this morning. The goal is to find three things they can use to symbolize their new youth-led group. These should include:

- something to stand for the feelings and ideas of individual group members (such as different leaves);
- something that reminds you of your group's past weaknesses (such as a broken branch to show lack of unity); and
- your greatest hope for your group's future (such as soft green moss to stand for warmth).

But this nature walk is different from others: you can't let go of your partners' hands. You have to go up and down stairs, through doors, over hills, around trees—everywhere—without letting go. This also means that only the group members at each end of the line can pick up or carry the symbols you find (though anyone can suggest ideas). The group may have to stop and talk about how to get past some obstacles without breaking the line and what to pick up. But that's the idea—to work together.

Have the group return at a set time or a signal. When the group has returned, have the line bend around to form a circle, but don't link ends. Have the teenagers at the ends of the line assemble group members' symbols according to the group's directions. Use the symbols in your worship setting later in the morning.

Debrief the experience by asking:

- How did they feel being so attached?
- What was fun? difficult?
- How is this experience like the youth group?

Then close by asking someone with a free hand to read aloud the parable of the yeast (Luke 13:20-21). Say: As children of God and part of his creation, how are we part of the yeast Jesus spoke about? As we conclude this retreat today and go home, we'll share the excitement of starting a new youth-led group in our church—a group that can grow and change just as we grow and change.

Then sing a favorite group song, and head off to breakfast—with the line still intact.

Worship—New Beginnings

This worship service marks the beginning of your year of youth-led meetings. This service is youth-led. Before the retreat, recruit youth council members to lead the service. Give them all the information they'll need for the service.

The service uses skits to tell the story of Jesus' life. At the end, the service symbolically sends the group out to share God's love. Just as Jesus' life and ministry brought new beginnings to the disciples' lives, his life also brings new beginnings to our lives today.

Ask group members to bring the sack of things they discovered on the nature scavenger hunt, their Bibles and pennies.

Call to worship. Start by having the group create its own worship setting. This could be an established outdoor worship setting or a setting someone has discovered during the weekend. If you need a table for banner supplies, carry a table along.

When you arrive at your worship site, divide into teams of five or six group members. Put banner-making and collage supplies on a table. Give each team about 30 minutes to make a felt banner, collage or display that symbolizes its feelings about the retreat and the youth group's new direction. Teams will share their creations later in the worship service. Encourage group members to use materials from the scavenger hunt.

Sing a new song. When all the creations are made, spend a few minutes singing favorite songs. Let group members suggest their favorites. Perhaps your group has learned a new song or adopted one as the group's favorite for the weekend. If you or a group member plays a guitar or other portable instrument, great. If not, just make a joyful noise.

Bible study. With the worship setting ready, divide your group into five new teams. Give each team a Bible, a Bible passage and a description of the skit. Explain that each team will perform a short skit based on the passage it's been given. Challenge teams to be creative in interpreting the passages' meanings. Allow about 15 minutes to prepare the following skits:

Skit 1: Jesus' birth and childhood (Luke 2:1-7)

Skit 2: Teaching through parables (Luke 10:25-37)

Skit 3: Jesus' travels and answers to questions (Matthew 25:42-45)

Skit 4: Jesus' Crucifixion (Matthew 26:17-75 and 27:11-56)

Skit 5: Jesus' Resurrection (Luke 24:1-12)

When group members are ready, have each team present its skit to the whole group. After all the skits, form a circle and ask group members to tell what stage of Jesus' life means the most to their lives.

Benediction: Covenant to new beginnings. Set at the front of your worship center the rainbow-shape banner you prepared before the retreat. If you're outside, put a piece of cardboard behind the banner to make it stiff enough to write on. Have different-color markers available.

Have all retreat participants (adults and teenagers) write the following on the banner in the shape and colors of a rainbow:

1. Name

2. Hopes for the youth group in the next year

3. One thing they're willing to give the new group each week

Have participants maintain the rainbow shape as they write with the different colors. (Keep this rainbow banner in your youth room as a reminder of the covenant you've made to each other and the new youth-led group.)

When participants have written on the rainbow, say: We have created a rainbow as a symbol of our promise to God and our youth group. May we remember our commitment through the coming year. Close with prayer, asking God to help us keep our promises or covenants with the same faithfulness that he has kept his covenant with us.

After the service, allow time for cleanup and packing before lunch.

Evaluation

Before you leave the retreat, allow about 15 minutes for participants to complete the retreat evaluation (Handout 2-6). If you wish, have participants discuss their feelings about the retreat. Close with prayer or a favorite song. Give group members time to gather their belongings before you head home.

Handout 2-5

Love Your Neighbor Puzzle

"Teacher, which is the greatest commandment in the law?"

Jesus replied: " 'Love the Lord your God with all your heart and with all your soul and with all your mind.' This is the first and greatest commandment. And the second is like it: 'Love your neighbor as yourself.' "

—Matthew 22:36-39

Retreat Evaluation

1. What did you like most about this retreat? _____
_____
_____
_____
_____

2. What did you dislike most?_____
_____
_____
_____
_____

3. What would you change about the weekend? Explain how you would do something differently. _____
_____
_____
_____
_____

4. What would you keep the same? _____
_____
_____
_____
_____

5. Other comments: _____
_____
_____
_____
_____

PART TWO:

Ready-to-Use Meeting Plans

Discovering Our Talents
MEETING 1

Young people usually think that having talent means that you're on the varsity sports team or that you're the most popular person in class. This meeting helps group members see that everyone has God-given talents. And it reminds us that sometimes we don't pay attention to the most important talents: inner gifts such as kindness, generosity, humility and love.

Objectives

In this meeting, group members will:
- discover unrecognized talents in themselves;
- play a game that helps them select important personal characteristics;
- learn that each person has good and bad traits, yet God cares for each person; and
- affirm each other for the unique gifts God gives each person.

Biblical Foundation

The Bible study points out that we each have both good and bad traits. But God accepts and loves us with all our imperfections, and he doesn't judge us harshly if we don't judge others harshly (Matthew 13:24-30 and Matthew 7:1-2).

Adult Leader's Responsibilities

1. Meet with the meeting coordinator two weeks ahead of time. Help him or her find group members to lead different aspects of the meeting.

2. Call leaders several days in advance to ask if they have any questions and to be sure they have gathered all supplies and have prepared adequately.

3. Make sure the leaders have an accurate count of how many people to expect at the meeting. Remind the leaders that it's better to have a few extra materials than not enough.

Meeting Coordinator's Responsibilities

1. Copy the instructions of each part of the meeting to give to the leaders.

2. At least two weeks before the meeting, find group members to lead different aspects of the meeting. (If you wish, you may lead one of the sections yourself.) Give leaders each a photocopy of the meeting element they're leading. Encourage leaders to find helpers if they need them.

3. Schedule a planning session one week before the event with all leaders to go through the meeting to be sure everyone understands it.

4. Find someone to coordinate refreshments for after the meeting.

5. The day before the meeting, call all the leaders to make sure they're ready for the meeting.

Meeting Outline				
Coordinator: _____				
Activity	**Estimated Time**	**Who's Responsible**	**Telephone**	**Confirmed**
Community-Builder: Talent Search	10 minutes			
Learning Time: Choosing Talents	20 minutes			
Bible Study: What God Sees in Us	30 minutes			
Closing: A Blue Ribbon Winner	10 minutes			
Refreshments				

COMMUNITY-BUILDER: Talent Search

What You'll Need

- ☐ Copies of "In Search of Myself" (Handout 1-1)
- ☐ Pencils
- ☐ Albums
- ☐ Stereo or tape player
- ☐ Chairs

Time Needed:

10 minutes

We often describe friends by what they do: "He's a football star"; "She's a cheerleader"; "He's on the debate team"; "She's club president." As a result, if you're not involved in those kinds of activities, you may feel insignificant. This activity emphasizes that every person has unique talents to contribute.

How to Prepare

1. Gather the supplies listed in the "What You'll Need" box.

2. Read the "How to Lead" section to be sure you understand the activity.

3. Photocopy Handout 1-1, "In Search of Myself" for each group member you expect at the meeting.

4. Set up the stereo or tape player to play background music as group members fill out their forms. Choose upbeat, positive albums that fit the idea that each person is important.

5. Arrange the chairs along the room's walls so group members can sit down and still have room to move around during the activity.

How to Lead

1. As group members arrive, have upbeat music playing on the stereo or tape player.

2. Give each person a pencil and a copy of the "In Search of Myself" handout. Have group members each begin completing their handout as soon as they arrive.

3. After group members have worked on their handouts for about five minutes, ask them to pair up with the person with whom they have the most in common. If three or more people share the same characteristics, have them join together in a team.

4. When everyone is with a partner, have the group form a circle of chairs. Have partners report on the characteristics they share. Ask the group:

● Did you discover something new about yourself through the activity? Explain.

● Were there any surprises for you in talking with other people? Explain.

● How did this activity make you feel about yourself and other people in the group?

In Search of Myself

Instructions

1. In the left-hand column, write the five best personality characteristics you have. For example, you could write: "kindness, honesty, thoughtfulness, friendliness and helpfulness." Don't be bashful. Be honest, and make a good list.

2. When you've filled out that column, find someone who has listed similar characteristics. Write that person's name in the second column, and place a checkmark by the characteristics you share.

3. Continue this process until you've talked with eight people.

Five Personality Characteristics	Person 1 Name: _____	Person 2 Name: _____	Person 3 Name: _____	Person 4 Name: _____	Person 5 Name: _____	Person 6 Name: _____	Person 7 Name: _____	Person 8 Name: _____
1.								
2.								
3.								
4.								
5.								

Choosing Talents

What You'll Need

- ☐ A hat, a set of "Talent Cards" and 10 blank cards for each group of five people
- ☐ Copies of "Talent Cards" (Handout 1-2)
- ☐ 3×5 cards
- ☐ Tape or glue
- ☐ Scissors
- ☐ Pencils
- ☐ Floor pillows or tables (optional)

Time Needed:

20 minutes

"I wish I could start over and be a totally different person!" Everyone feels like saying that sometimes. We all wish we could be someone who's well-liked, talented and special. The truth is, we're all special already. We all have unique talents. In this activity, group members will discover their special talents.

How to Prepare

1. Gather the supplies listed in the "What You'll Need" box. Find a variety of hats—any style will work.

2. Prepare the "Talent Cards" by photocopying Handout 1-2, cutting out the individual boxes and taping or gluing them to 3×5 cards. Make enough sets of talent cards (30 in each set) for every five people to have a complete set. For example, if you expect 15 people at your meeting, you'll need three sets. Add 10 blank 3×5 cards to each set.

3. Read the "How to Lead" section to be sure you understand the activity.

4. Clear floor space or have small tables where teams of five can play the game. If you want, bring floor pillows to make sitting on the floor more comfortable.

How to Lead

1. After the community-builder, have group members form teams of five. If you have extra people, form another small team.

2. Have each team find a place to play. Then give each team a hat, a set of 40 cards (including 10 blank cards) and pencils.

3. When everyone is settled, explain the rules:

● The game's object is to end up with two cards that answer two questions:

a. What is most important in life to you?

b. What do you most want to achieve in your life?

● To begin, one person deals everyone six cards—four Talent Cards and two blank cards. Shuffle the remaining 10 Talent Cards, and place them face down in the hat.

● Each player can only hold five cards at a time. Therefore, you must first discard one card before playing. Place it face up on the table.

● When everyone has discarded his or her card, go around the team clockwise. You have three choices of what to do:

a. Draw a new card out of the hat;

b. Pick a card shown on the table; or

c. Write a different characteristic on a blank card.

● Since you can only have five cards at a time, you must discard a card before you pick a new card from the hat or table.

● When you have collected the two best cards, get rid of all the others. You can only discard one card at a time.

● The first person to discard all the extra cards wins the game.

4. When all the teams have finished playing, bring the whole group together. Have each team report on its experience. Ask the following questions:

● Why did you choose the particular characteristics you selected?

● Which talents do you think are most important in life? Explain.

● What kinds of talents can you keep throughout your life, and which ones can you lose?

● Are the important talents ones that only a few people have, or can anyone have them? Explain.

Talent Cards

Instructions:
Cut along the lines to make 30 talent cards. Tape or glue each box to a separate 3 × 5 card. Make one set of cards for every five group members you expect at your meeting.

Sophisticated	Sense of humor	Athletic	Musically talented	Beautiful
Smart	Reliable	Happy	Artistic	Honest
Responsible	Humble	Loving	Healthy	Confident
Talented	Sexy	A winner	Polite	Famous
Rich	Kind	Compassionate	Helpful	Friendly
Cooperative	Popular	Grateful	Creative	Accepting

What God Sees in Us

Do you judge people who you don't even know? Unfortunately, we all do. When we see people for the first time, we often judge them based on how they're dressed, whether they're tall or thin, if they seem shy or talkative, or how they measure up to some other superficial standard.

What would happen if God judged us the same way we judge other people? This Bible study looks at what God values in us.

What You'll Need

☐ Bibles
☐ Paper and pencils
☐ Copies of "Wheat and Weeds" (Handout 1-3)

Time Needed:

30 minutes

How to Prepare

1. Gather the supplies listed in the "What You'll Need" box.
2. Read the "How to Lead" section to be sure you understand the activity.
3. Make enough copies of Handout 1-3, "Wheat and Weeds," for everyone.

How to Lead

1. Give everyone a copy of Handout 1-3, a pencil and a Bible.
2. Ask group members to read Matthew 13:24-30, the Parable of the Weeds. Then have group members each complete the "For Individual Reflection" section on the handout. Allow about five minutes.
3. When people have finished their lists, form teams of five. Have each team designate a discussion leader.
4. Give teams each a sheet of paper. Ask each team to make a master list of characteristics that are pleasing to God (the wheat) and ones that are upsetting to God (the weeds), based on their charts. Allow about five minutes.
5. Then ask each team to discuss the questions on Handout 1-3. Encourage someone on each team to take notes to report to the whole group. Allow about 10 minutes.
6. When teams have finished with the questions, bring everyone together in a circle. Ask each team to report briefly on its discussion.
7. After all teams have reported, read Matthew 7:1-2 aloud. Ask people to think of how the passage relates to the discussion of wheat and weeds. Ask:
● What does this passage say about how we should respond when we see "weeds" in other people's lives?
● When we judge others, are we actually judging ourselves as the passage suggests? In what ways?
● How can we shift our perspective so we don't focus on other people's faults but on the inner gifts God has given them?

Wheat and Weeds

For Individual Reflection
1. Read Matthew 13:24-30, the Parable of the Weeds. Then, in the following chart, list five good qualities in people that are like the wheat in the parable and five bad qualities that are like the weeds.

Qualities Like the Wheat	Qualities Like the Weeds
1.	1.
2.	2.
3.	3.
4.	4.
5.	5.

2. Look at the list you wrote and think about which of these qualities you see in yourself. Check (✓) those qualities in both columns.

For Group Discussion
1. If you rewrote the list to focus on the characteristics many people say are important, how would the list differ from a list of "wheat" and "weeds" based on scripture?

2. Do you think we're all good or all bad? Or is there a mixture of wheat and weeds in all of us? Explain your answer.

3. Do you think God will accept us if we're a mixture of wheat and weeds? Explain.

4. Which do we tend to emphasize in ourselves—wheat or weeds? Why do you think we do this?

5. What are some ways you nurture the "wheat" in your life in order to choke out the "weeds"?

What You'll Need

☐ Materials to make blue ribbons (construction paper, blue ribbon, scissors, stapler)
☐ Pencils or markers
☐ Recording of victory songs (such as the Olympic Games theme song or "We Are the World")
☐ Stool or block to stand on
☐ Stereo or tape player

Time Needed:

10 minutes

Sample 1-4

Blue Ribbon

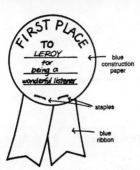

Most of us dream of having our name called as the winner at the swim meet, bake-off, spelling bee or other contest. But we can all be "winners" in life by trying to be the best people we can be. This activity lets you give yourself a blue ribbon for your efforts to love and accept others.

How to Prepare

1. Gather the supplies listed in the "What You'll Need" box.

2. Read the "How to Lead" section to be sure you understand the activity.

3. Make blue ribbons to award to everyone at the meeting. They can be simple blue ribbons stapled to blue construction paper circles that say "First Place" (see Sample 1-4). Leave room for group members to write on the badge.

4. Choose victory music to play while group members write their awards. The theme from the Olympic Games or a celebration song such as "We Are the World" would be appropriate.

5. Make sure a tape player or stereo is available to play the music.

How to Lead

1. After the Bible study, have group members sit in a circle. Give each person a blue ribbon and a marker or pencil.

2. Say: You're sitting by a winner! No matter who's sitting next to you, that person has important gifts and talents. On your blue ribbon, write one thing about the person on your left that you consider a positive talent.

Remember, we're not talking about talents like sports or music. We're talking about gifts we've been given as followers of Christ: being kind, being a good listener, being easy to talk to, being helpful or being a good friend. Think beyond the obvious and give your blue ribbon for something special about that person.

3. Give group members time to write on their ribbons. Play your victory music as they write.

4. Then announce that it's time for your awards ceremony. Ask group members each to present their ribbon to their neighbor and explain the award to the group. Have the person being "awarded" stand on a block or stool like an awards platform at the Olympics. Begin by giving an example yourself. You might say, "I award Andrea this blue ribbon for being such a sincere listener." Then ask for volunteers by saying, "Who would like to present their blue ribbon next?" Give everyone a chance.

5. Encourage group members to clap and cheer wildly after each presentation—just as you would at any other contest. Turn up the music between presentations to add to the enthusiasm.

6. When everyone has presented a ribbon, close the meeting with circle prayer. Have group members hold hands. Ask them to say one-word or sentence prayers, thanking God for a gift he has given them. Announce that it's time for a victory feast—otherwise known as refreshments.

True Friendship

Friendship is important to teenagers. They're in the process of discovering who they are, and part of that discovery involves working out their relationships with other people.

Sometimes, though, friendships are based on superficial values. And teenagers sometimes think the only way they can be true friends is to act or dress exactly like other people. This meeting stresses that true friendship is based on the kind of people we are, not on how we dress or look. The meeting challenges your group to welcome everyone.

Objectives

In this meeting, group members will:
- look at the types of friends they are to other people;
- play a game that examines the attributes of true friends;
- examine Bible passages about friendship; and
- express their friendship for each other.

Biblical Foundation

The following Bible passages will be used to highlight the qualities of Christian friendship: John 15:12-14; James 4:4; Proverbs 18:24; 1 Corinthians 13:4-10; Matthew 7:1-2; Matthew 5:7; and Ephesians 4:25-32.

Adult Leader's Responsibilities

1. Meet with the meeting coordinator two weeks ahead of time. Help him or her find group members to lead each aspect of the meeting.

2. Call leaders several days in advance to ask if they have any questions and to be sure they've gathered all supplies and prepared adequately. Assist the "Friendship Maze" leader in preparing the game boards.

Meeting Coordinator's Responsibilities

1. Copy the instructions of each part of the meeting to give to the leaders.

2. At least two weeks before the meeting, find group members to lead each aspect of the meeting. (If you wish, you may lead one of the sections yourself.) Give leaders each a photocopy of the meeting element they're leading. Encourage leaders to find helpers.

3. Schedule a planning session one week before the event with all leaders to go through the meeting to be sure everyone understands it.

4. Find someone to coordinate refreshments for after the meeting. You might suggest gingerbread-man cookies, which look like the friendship chain in the discussion-starter.

5. The day before the meeting, call all the leaders to make sure they're ready.

Meeting Outline				
Coordinator: _____				
Activity	**Estimated Time**	**Who's Responsible**	**Telephone**	**Confirmed**
Community-Builder: What Kind of Friend Am I?	10 minutes			
Discussion-Starter: Friendship Maze	20 minutes			
Bible Study: To Be a Friend	15 minutes			
Affirmation: Friendship Bracelets	10 minutes			
Closing: The Friendship Connection	5 minutes			
Refreshments				

COMMUNITY-BUILDER: What Kind of Friend Am I?

What You'll Need

- ☐ Kitchen utensils such as wooden spoons, garlic presses, spatulas, mixers, saltshakers, pot holders, rolling pins, spoons, can openers, strainers and so forth.
- ☐ Circle of chairs
- ☐ Table

Time Needed:

10 minutes

If someone asked you, "What kind of friend are you?" how would you answer? Would you have to stop and think? This community-builder asks group members to think about themselves as friends.

How to Prepare

1. Gather the supplies listed in the "What You'll Need" box either from home or your church kitchen. Don't include knives or anything that could hurt someone. Collect more items than you actually need for your group, so everyone will have a choice.

2. Read the "How to Lead" section to be sure you understand the activity.

3. Arrange a circle of chairs in the meeting room—not around a table.

4. Set a table off to the side. Spread the kitchen items on it.

How to Lead

1. When it's time to start the meeting, say: What kind of friend do you consider yourself to be? To answer that question, I'm going to ask you to choose a kitchen item that you feel symbolizes the type of friend you are.

For example, I might pick up a tea strainer because I have lots of friends, and I find it difficult to have one best friend.

Then continue: Everyone go to the table and choose a utensil. When you find your item, bring it back to the circle. Remind everyone that you want them to take the experience seriously.

2. When group members have their items, give each of them a chance to tell what they selected and why. Respond positively after each person speaks. You might say: That's great. I like how you used the salt in the saltshaker to represent different friends.

Encourage people to volunteer by saying: Who'd like to share next? or I'm really curious about what that garlic press reminded you of. Encourage group members to volunteer instead of going around the circle. Volunteering lets everyone feel more in control, and they don't feel pressured.

3. When everyone has shared, ask the group to help you think of "the most important quality of a good friend."

4. Ask group members to return the utensils to the table.

Friendship Maze

What You'll Need

- ☐ A "Friendship Maze" game board for each group of 6 people (Handout 2-1)
- ☐ A rule sheet for each game board (Handout 2-2)
- ☐ A set of 3×5 number cards for each board
- ☐ Scissors
- ☐ 8½×14 paper for friendship chains
- ☐ Pencils and markers
- ☐ Newsprint
- ☐ Self-adhesive plastic (optional)
- ☐ A basket full of miscellaneous game tokens— such as coins, peanuts, old keys, paper clips, tiny toys, pen caps, spools of thread or small crayon pieces (one per person)
- ☐ Tables

Time Needed:

20 minutes

If someone asked about our best friend, we'd all say something different. And some of us wouldn't know what to say because we may feel like most of our friends are "acquaintances," not "best friends." We all have different ideas of what a friend is. The "Friendship Maze" board gives students a chance to each write their own definition of a true friend.

 ## How to Prepare

1. Make the "Friendship Maze" game boards (Handout 2-1) so you have one board for every six people. You can enlarge the boards with a photocopier or ask a copy shop to enlarge them to about 11×24 on heavy card stock. If you enlarge them on paper, attach them to cardboard for sturdiness.

You may want to decorate the game boards using colored markers. Cover the boards with self-adhesive plastic to protect the surface so they will last longer. The game can be reused on retreats, during game nights at the church, or any time group members have a chance to sit down and play with friends.

2. Make a set of six number cards for each game board, using 3×5 cards. Lightly write the numbers (1, 2, 3, 4, 5, 6) on each set. Be sure the numbers don't show through on the other side.

3. Gather the supplies listed in the "What You'll Need" box.

4. Photocopy the "Friendship Maze Game Rules" (Handout 2-2) for each game board.

5. At the top of a sheet of newsprint, write: "A friend is someone who . . ."

6. Read the "How to Lead" section and the "Friendship Maze Game Rules" to be sure you understand the game. Practice cutting out paper-doll friendship chains so you can show a sample chain to the group (Sample 2-3).

7. Play the game with two or three friends to be sure you understand it.

8. Have floor space cleared or tables set up where teams can play. They'll need enough room to spread out their friendship chains. Set up the board games. Put a set of number cards, pencils and a rules sheet with each board.

 ## How to Lead

1. After the community-builder, have group members number off into groups of about six people each. Ask each group to go to a game board.

2. Let students each pick a token from the basket that symbolizes their friendship style. Also give each person a sheet of paper, scissors and a pencil or marker.

3. Have everyone make a paper-doll friendship chain. Demonstrate as you explain how to do it. (Keep extra paper on hand in case someone cuts the wrong way. Offer to help anyone who has trouble.)
- Make five fan-like folds in your paper.
- Cut a doll shape to make a chain of paper dolls holding hands. Everyone should have five dolls in the chain.
- Don't write anything on the chain before the game.

4. Carefully explain the game directions so everyone understands. Then begin the game. Go around to each board answering questions.

5. After the game, bring the whole group together in a circle. Have group members each show and explain their friendship chain.

6. Conclude the activity by posting the "A friend is someone who . . ." newsprint. Ask group members each to suggest one quality that's essential in a definition of a friend. Write these qualities on the newsprint.

Friendship Maze Game Rules

Your goal in this game is to fill your paper-doll chain with 10 qualities you think are important in friendship. Here's how it works:

1. All players put their tokens on the square marked "ENTER MAZE HERE."

2. To start the game, each player draws one number card. The person with the lowest number then moves his or her token in either direction, the number of spaces specified on the card. (So if you draw a five, you could move clockwise five spaces to land on "Non-judgmental.")

3. If you land on a space that lists a personal quality, you have two options:
● If you think it's an important friendship quality, write it on your friendship chain.
● If you don't think it's important, don't write anything.

4. If you land on spaces that don't list personal qualities, here's what happens:
● **One-way space:** You may only move in the direction indicated until the end of the game.
● **Occupied space:** Go back 10 spaces.
● **Free space:** Think of an important friendship quality that's not on the board, and write it on your friendship chain.

5. When everyone has played once, collect and shuffle the number cards. Have each person draw again; then go around the circle again in turn.

6. The first person to enter the center circle on the game board with 10 important qualities written on their friendship chain wins. However, you cannot enter the center circle unless you've collected 10 important qualities. If you enter the center circle before you collect them, go backward on your next turn until you collect the necessary qualities. Then head back to the center circle.

Sample 2-3

Paper-Doll Chain

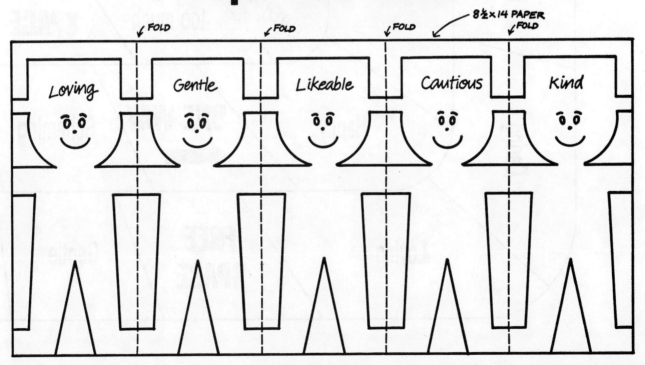

Kind　Smart　Tolerant　Coope

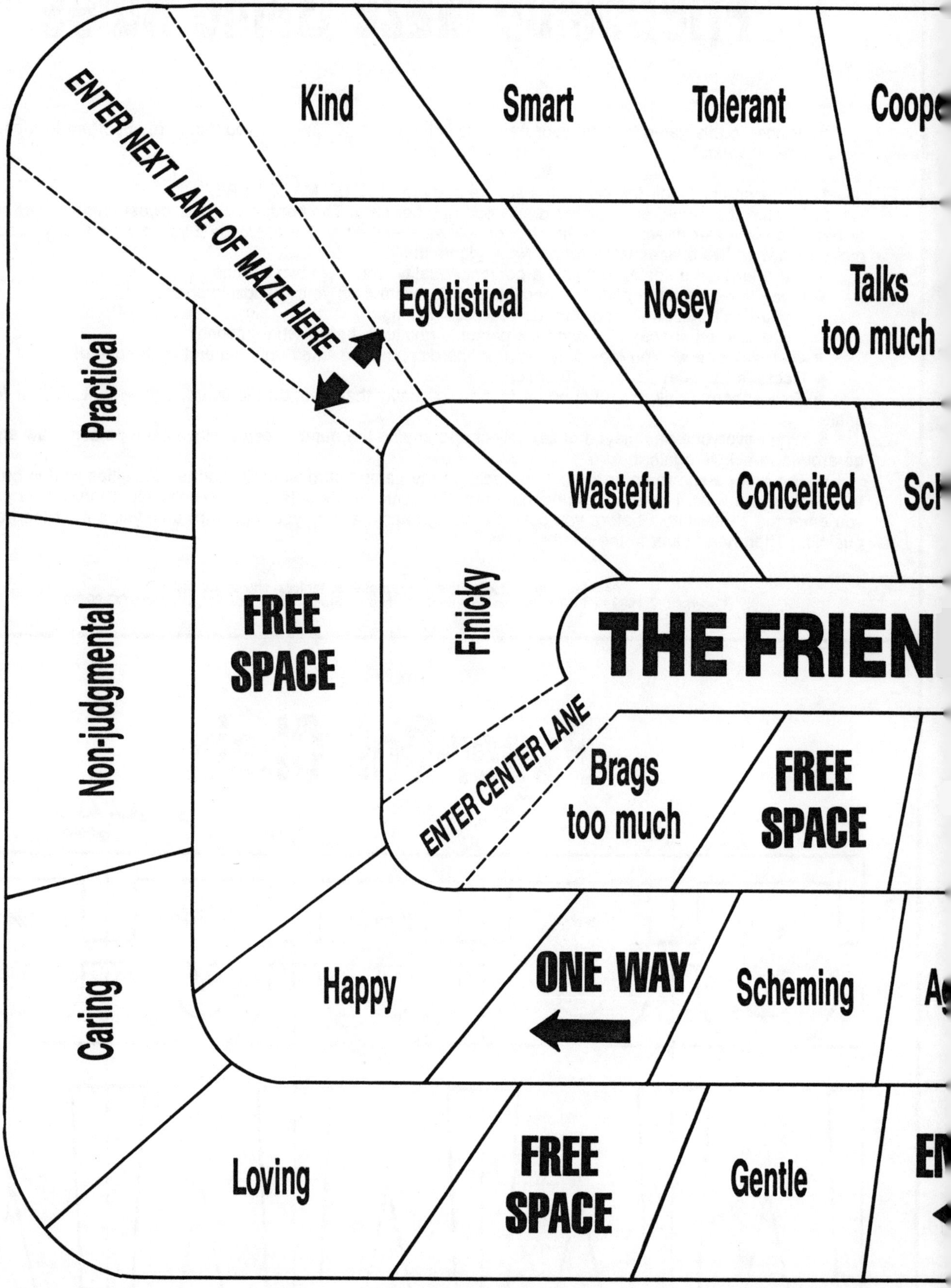

ENTER NEXT LANE OF MAZE HERE

Egotistical　Nosey　Talks too much

Practical

Wasteful　Conceited　Sch

Finicky

Non-judgmental

FREE SPACE

THE FRIEN

ENTER CENTER LANE

Brags too much　FREE SPACE

Caring　Happy　ONE WAY　Scheming　Ag

Loving　FREE SPACE　Gentle　EN

Creative

Keeps promises

FREE SPACE

Reliable

Active

NE WAY

Helpless

FREE SPACE

ENTER NEXT LANE HERE

Understanding

Demanding

Sloppy

SLOW DOWN— SIT OUT ONE TURN

Cautious

SHIP MAZE

ish

Greedy

Stingy

Sympathetic

ssive

Listens Well

STOP RETURN TO START

Reckless

R MAZE ERE ➔

Likeable

Generous

Truthful

BIBLE STUDY: # To Be a Friend

What You'll Need

- ☐ 14 small brown paper lunch bags
- ☐ 3×5 cards
- ☐ Collage supplies such as old magazines and various markers
- ☐ bottles of glue
- ☐ Several pairs of scissors
- ☐ Bibles
- ☐ Tables

Time Needed:

15 minutes

Collages can be fun to make, and they can help explain what something means. The Bible study revolves around making collage blocks based on seven Bible passages about friendship. The collage blocks help explore the Bible and interpret what it says to us today about our friendships.

 ## How to Prepare

1. Gather the supplies listed in the "What You'll Need" box.

2. Read the "How to Lead" section to be sure you understand the activity. Practice making a collage block before the meeting so you can show the group a sample.

3. Write each of the following Bible references on 3×5 cards:

- John 15:12-14
- Proverbs 18:24
- Matthew 7:1-2
- Ephesians 4:25-32
- James 4:4
- 1 Corinthians 13:4-10
- Matthew 5:7

4. Put the Bible reference cards in seven separate paper bags. (You'll still have seven empty ones.)

5. Set up a collage supply table and tables where teams can make collage blocks. Load the supply table with plenty of collage supplies.

 ## How to Lead

1. After the Friendship Maze game, divide your group into seven teams. If the group is small, you might end up with only one or two people in each group.

2. Give each team two small brown paper lunch bags—one containing a Bible verse and the other empty. Also distribute Bibles.

3. Ask each team to read its Bible passage and make a collage block explaining the passage. Give teams about 10 minutes to finish.

Here's how to make a collage block:

- Cover each side and the bottom of one paper bag with pictures. Cut pictures from magazines, draw pictures or combine the two. Then cover only the bottom of the second bag. Include the Bible verse itself in the design.

- When the designs are complete, open both paper bags. Place the bag that has pictures only on the bottom inside the other bag top-into-top. The two bags together make a paper block that's covered with pictures.

4. When all the teams are finished, bring the whole group back together in a circle. Ask someone from each group to read the passage and to explain the team's collage.

Friendship Bracelets

AFFIRMATION:

What You'll Need

- □ 1×8½ strips of construction paper
- □ Pencils
- □ Tape

Time Needed:

10 minutes

Everyone needs to hear kind, positive words from friends. This activity gives group members the opportunity to share kind words with other group members.

How to Prepare

1. Cut 1×8½ strips of colored construction paper before the meeting. Gather the other supplies listed in the "What You'll Need" box.

2. Make a friendship bracelet as an example.

3. Read the "How to Lead" section to be sure you understand the activity.

How to Lead

1. After the collage-block share time, ask group members to stay in the circle. Give everyone a pencil and a strip of paper.

2. Have group members each write their name on their paper. Then ask them each to pass their strip around the circle, beginning with the person on their right.

3. As the papers are passed, everyone writes on the paper strip a positive friendship quality he or she recognizes in the person. Stress that students should write only positive comments.

4. When the paper strips return to their owners, give people a chance to read their friends' comments.

5. Ask group members each to fold their paper into a thin strip (about half an inch wide). Tape the two ends together around each student's arm to make a bracelet. Encourage students to wear the friendship bracelets home.

The Friendship Connection

What You'll Need

☐ A ball of string
☐ Scissors
☐ Recording of a friendship song; stereo or tape player (optional)

Time Needed:

5 minutes

Your youth group is a good place to begin helping group members feel like they have friends. This closing activity re-emphasizes the meaning of friendship and stresses friendships within the group.

 ## How to Prepare

1. Gather the supplies listed in the "What You'll Need" box.
2. Read the "How to Lead" section to be sure you understand the activity.
3. Practice what you want to say to the group to conclude the meeting on friendship. You can use the wording in #4 under "How to Lead," or think of something that would be particularly appropriate for your group.
4. Select a song about friendship that everyone knows. If possible, find someone to accompany the group as you sing the song. Otherwise, sing a capella, or find a recording of a popular friendship song to play for the group.

 ## How to Lead

1. Start the closing right after the affirmation time. Stay seated in your big circle.
2. Holding one end of the string in your hand, pass the ball around the circle. Have each person hold onto the string as he or she passes the ball around.
3. When the ball comes back to you, cut the string and tie the two loose ends together.
4. Then say: Within this circle, we're all friends. And, like the string, our friendship makes us one big circle of friends. At the same time, we're still individuals within that circle. We don't all have to be alike, act alike or dress alike to be friends. We can all be friends with each other because we're all part of God's family.
5. Next, use the scissors to cut the string between you and the person on your right. As you cut the string, tell one way you act that you think encourages others to want to be friends with you. You might say, for example, "I think my willingness to listen to other people helps them want to be my friend."
6. Then pass the scissors to the group member on your right, and have that person repeat #5.
7. When you've gone around the circle, ask students each to tie their string through a buttonhole or belt loop as a reminder of their friendships.
8. Join hands and sing (or listen to) a song about friendship.
9. Close with prayer or your group's traditional closing.

Reaching Out to People in Need

We see hungry people on the news and on our streets. We want to help them, but we don't know how. So we throw up our hands and say, "What difference can I make?"

Christ calls on all his followers to help people in need. This meeting presents some ways each person can make a difference.

Objectives

In this meeting, group members will:
- discover the limitations of donations to food banks;
- explore Bible passages about sharing with people in need; and
- find ways they can contribute responsibly to help people in need.

Biblical Foundation

Dozens of scripture passages focus on Christians' responsibility to the poor. This meeting focuses on Matthew 6:2-4; Matthew 25:34-40; Luke 6:34-35; 1 Corinthians 16:2; and 2 Corinthians 9:6.

Adult Leader's Responsibilities

1. Meet with the meeting coordinator at least three weeks in advance. Help the coordinator find a group member to lead each aspect of the meeting. Have the coordinator arrange a meeting with the leaders to coordinate efforts two weeks in advance.

2. A week before the meeting, call each leader to be sure everyone is getting ready.

3. Help the Learning Time leader collect information and brochures about the different relief organizations.

Meeting Coordinator's Responsibilities

1. Make a copy of the instructions for each part of the meeting to give to the leaders.

2. At least three weeks before the meeting, find a group member to lead each aspect of the meeting. (If you wish, you may lead one of the sections yourself.) Give leaders each a photocopy of the meeting element they're leading. Encourage leaders to find helpers.

3. Schedule a planning session with all leaders two weeks before the event to go through the meeting and be sure everyone understands it.

4. Find someone to coordinate refreshments. One suggestion would be to have a Third World meal that consists of only a little rice, beans and water. Then emphasize to the group that what you served as a snack is more than many people eat in a whole day.

5. The day before the meeting, call all the leaders to make sure they're ready.

Meeting Outline				
Coordinator: _____				
Activity	Estimated Time	Who's Responsible	Telephone	Confirmed
Community-Builder: Fill the Basket	10 minutes			
Discussion-Starter: Food for Thought	10 minutes			
Bible Study: Sharing Charades	15 minutes			
Learning Time: How to Help	25 minutes			
Closing: I Can Make a Difference	10 minutes			
Refreshments				

COMMUNITY-BUILDER: Fill the Basket

What You'll Need

- [ ] A bushel basket or cardboard box
- [ ] Paper and pencils
- [ ] Plastic forks, spoons and knives (an equal number of each). You'll need enough so that each person can have either a knife, fork or spoon.
- [ ] Tables and chairs

Time Needed:

10 minutes

Most churches collect food for people in need. But what do we donate? Extras from our pantries? Whatever is on sale? Everything we donate is desperately needed. But why don't we donate the kinds of food we want on our own tables? In this activity, group members will discover how hard it is to plan nutritious meals from random food donations.

How to Prepare

1. Two weeks before the meeting, announce that you'll have a food drive beginning at your next youth group meeting. Ask group members to bring nonperishable foods to donate to needy people in your community. Put a notice in the church newsletter and bulletin so everyone will know.

2. Read the "How to Lead" section to be sure you understand the activity.

3. Gather the supplies listed in the "What You'll Need" box.

4. Set up tables ahead of time for each team to plan its menu and shopping list.

5. If you wish, decorate the basket or cardboard box for donations. Put the basket or box on a table near the youth room door.

How to Lead

1. As group members arrive, have them put the nonperishable foods they brought in the basket or box near the door. Then give each person either a knife, fork or spoon. Alternate what you give so that you distribute an equal number of each utensil. Ask each person to keep his or her utensil for the whole meeting.

2. When it's time to start, divide the group into three teams by asking group members to get together with others who have the same utensil. (Forks get with forks, knives with knives, and spoons with spoons.) Have each team gather at a different table.

3. When teams are at their tables, say: Your job is to plan a meal for a family of four. It needs to be a balanced meal, something nutritious and tasty. Spoons, you plan breakfast. Forks, you plan lunch. Knives, you plan supper. (Give each team paper and pencils to write its menu. Allow about five minutes.)

4. When teams have planned their menus, ask each to write a shopping list of everything needed to prepare the meal. Allow about five minutes.

5. When all the teams have finished their lists, have them each send someone shopping to the basket or box of donated non-perishable food. Tell the shoppers to try and find everything on their lists to prepare their meals.

6. While the three are shopping, bring the remaining group members back together. Have the shoppers report on how successful they were at the "store."

Food for Thought

What You'll Need

☐ Copies of "Food for Thought" (Handout 3-1)
☐ Pencils

Time Needed:

10 minutes

The community-builder before this activity raises lots of questions about ways we try to help people in need. This discussion-starter time gives group members a chance to ask and discuss some of those questions.

 How to Prepare

1. Photocopy Handout 3-1, "Food for Thought." You'll need one copy for every three group members at the meeting.

2. Gather the supplies listed in the "What You'll Need" box.

3. Read the "How to Lead" section to be sure you understand the activity.

4. Ask your pastor or youth worker about your church or community food bank. Find out how much food it collects each year, how many people use it and what kinds of supplies the bank needs to provide balanced diets for people in need. Plan what you'll tell the youth group about what you learned.

 How to Lead

1. After hearing the reports from the "shoppers," say: Now we're going to form teams of "place settings" to discuss some questions. Get together with the other "utensils" you'd need to form a complete place setting. For example, if you're a fork, find a knife and spoon to form a small group.

2. Give group members time to form their teams of three. Then distribute Handout 3-1, "Food for Thought" and pencils to each group for discussion. Allow about five minutes.

3. When the teams have completed the worksheet, bring the whole group together to discuss the questions.

4. Tell what you learned about your community food bank's work and needs. Decide whether your group wants to help this effort, or to follow up this activity by actually raising money or collecting the food to feed a family for a day or week. Ask for volunteers to organize the project.

5. The food collected at this meeting can be the beginning of your own collection, or you can donate it to your local food bank.

Food for Thought

As a team, think about the following questions in light of the menus and shopping lists you planned for one day, and the success you had "shopping" in the basket of donated food.

1. How did it make you feel when you realized that you couldn't plan balanced meals from the donated food?

2. Do you think it's hard for people to plan nutritious meals from donated food? Why or why not?

3. Do you think it's easier for people in need to plan balanced meals if churches and other organizations combine their donations in a community food bank? Or is it better just to collect random contributions? Think of reasons to support your answer.

4. Should poor people have the same quality meals as other people in our society? Why or why not?

5. What are three specific ways our youth group could help people in poverty eat better meals?

a.

b.

c.

BIBLE STUDY: Sharing Charades

What You'll Need

- ☐ Bibles
- ☐ Copies of "Sharing Charades" (Handout 3-2)
- ☐ An offering plate or basket
- ☐ Newsprint
- ☐ Markers
- ☐ A watch (with a second hand) or a stopwatch

Time Needed:

15 minutes

When we think of helping others, we often think of missionaries overseas. But people are also in need right in our own neighborhoods. Many communities have organizations that prepare hot meals for the elderly, repair homes for people in poverty or meet other needs. Your youth group can help with the projects—even if you just help paint a house or build new porch steps for people who can't do it themselves. The "Sharing Charades" game will help you put the scriptures into practice by thinking of ways to help people today.

How to Prepare

1. Gather the supplies listed in the "What You'll Need" box.

2. Read the "How to Lead" section to be sure you understand the activity.

3. Make two copies of Handout 3-2, "Sharing Charades." Keep one copy to refer to during the activity. Then cut out the strips on the other copy and fold them in half to hide the writing. Put them in an offering plate or basket.

4. Read the Bible verses on the "Sharing Charades" paper strips so you're familiar with their contents.

5. Have newsprint and markers ready at the front of the meeting room.

How to Lead

1. After the discussion-starter, form new teams of four people each. To do this, have group members each find one other person with their utensil. Then these pairs find another pair with a *different* utensil. (If you have extra people, some teams can have five players.)

2. Post the newsprint at the front of the room where teams will be performing their charades. Tear off one sheet on which to keep score.

3. When group members are in a team, have each team choose two members to be "actors." The other two group members will guess what situation the actors are portraying.

4. Then say: We're going to play "Sharing Charades." When it's your team's turn, I'll let the two actors in your team pick out a strip from the offering plate. Each strip has a Bible reference and a situation on it. The actors have one minute to read the Bible verse and situation and to figure out how to act out the situation without talking. Then the actors write the Bible reference on newsprint and act out the situation. The other two team members try to guess what's being acted out. They may look up the Bible reference for clues.

For example: If you were acting out Matthew 5:42, one person could be a volunteer worker coming to your home, knocking and asking for a donation to help fight a disease. The other actor could then pretend to write a check and give it to the volunteer.

You have only one minute to guess, so work quickly. Sometimes it's quicker for one person to look up the verse while the other person figures out the situation. If you guess correctly within the minute, your team gets five points. If you don't guess right, the other teams have a chance to guess. If another team guesses correctly, that team gets one point.

Conclude by saying: Here's one final hint: Every situation in the game is something we could actually do as a youth group to help people, such as collecting food or giving money.

5. To start the game, get a team to volunteer by asking, "Who's hungry?" Say to the first person who raises a hand: Okay, your team can go first. Let the team's actors take a strip from the offering plate. Allow about one minute to prepare.

6. When the minute is up, tell the actors to write their Bible reference on newsprint and then begin acting—without talking. The other two team members have one minute to guess. Urge the "audience" not to give any clues.

7. If the guessing players are right, give their team five points. If they aren't, give the other teams a chance. If another team guesses correctly, it receives one point. Refer to a copy of the "Sharing Charades" handout to judge whether the team has guessed correctly. Keep track of each team's score on newsprint.

8. When you've discovered the situation, move quickly to the next team. Have teams do charades until all have participated. If your group is small, have teams switch roles so everyone has a chance to act.

9. Total each team's score, and lead a round of applause for the winning team.

Sharing Charades

Matthew 6:2-4
Contribute anonymously to a charity instead of donating through a TV program on which your name is announced.

Matthew 25:34-35
Collect food to give to hungry people in your neighborhood.

Matthew 25:36
Buy new clothes for a teenager whose parents can't afford to buy them.

1 Corinthians 16:2
Set aside part of your paycheck or allowance to give to people in need.

2 Corinthians 9:6
Give because you can and want to. Don't grumble about giving away money you were saving for a new album.

Matthew 25:37
Raise money to help underdeveloped countries drill new wells for clean drinking water.

Matthew 25:38
Bring blankets to the church to distribute to poor children to keep them warm this winter.

Matthew 25:39
Raise money for medical supplies that doctors can use around the world to help people who don't have medical care.

Matthew 25:40
Go to a low-income neighborhood and help repaint a garage for an elderly couple.

Luke 6:34-35
Help everyone—not just people you know, but also people you'll probably never meet.

How to Help

What You'll Need

- ☐ Information brochures about five hunger relief organizations (three or more copies of each)
- ☐ Newsprint with evaluation questions
- ☐ Two tables

Time Needed:

25 minutes

Many people wonder if the money they donate to charity actually gets to the people who need it. This activity helps you examine five organizations and gives your group a chance to plan its own mission project.

 ## How to Prepare

1. Three weeks before the meeting, collect at least three information brochures about each of five different relief organizations. Ask your pastor or youth minister about possible denominational, local and national organizations. Or write to some of the national organizations listed in Handout 3-3, "Hunger Relief Organizations." Select a variety of organizations that concentrate on different needs—emergency food, medical supplies or long-term development. Ask each organization for at least three brochures. (Most groups will be happy to give you more brochures to distribute to interested people.)

2. Pick five friends to help with this activity. Each friend will represent one of the organizations you selected, giving a one-minute introduction to the organization. Introductions should include:
- the type of relief or development work the organization does; and
- the advantages of the organization.

3. Give "representatives" each the brochures you collected about "their" organization.

4. Gather the materials listed in the "What You'll Need" box.

5. Read the "How to Lead" section to be sure you understand the activity.

6. Write the following questions on newsprint to help teams evaluate different organizations:
- What percentage of the money contributed to the organization goes directly into relief and development funds, and what percentage covers office expenses?
- Does the organization concentrate on long-term solutions to hunger problems—such as teaching farming skills or drilling wells for clean water? Or does the organization concentrate on emergency relief?
- Are there projects that your youth group can do through the organization to help people in your community, the nation or overseas?

7. Call the "representatives" two days before the meeting to remind them of their role and to see if they have any questions.

 ## How to Lead

1. After the "Sharing Charades," gather group members together. Then, form two teams by going around the circle with people alternately saying "hungry" or "not hungry." Then have the "hungries" go to one table and the "not hungries" go to the other. (If your group is larger than 20, you may want to form three groups.)

2. Explain that each team will pretend to be a youth council that decides what relief organization to support for a mission project. Tell each team that you've invited representatives from several organizations to make short presentations.

3. Introduce the five "representatives" as though they were official representatives. As each is introduced, he or she gives a one-minute presentation.

4. Give each "council" a brochure about each organization. Then give each team five minutes to:
- pick one organization to support for the summer mission project; and
- decide on a project to do within the next few months to support the cho-

sen organization.

5. Post the newsprint with questions to help teams evaluate the different groups. Tell teams to be ready to make a proposal to the whole group in two minutes.

6. After five minutes, bring the teams together in a circle. Have each team make its proposal. Discuss what group members like best about each project.

7. Conclude the discussion by deciding as a group if you're interested in actually doing the selected mission project. Ask for volunteers to organize the project.

Handout 3-3

Hunger Relief Organizations

CARE, 660 First Avenue, New York, NY 10016. (212) 686-3110. Works in Third World countries to help the world's poor and victims of disasters.

Christian Children's Fund, 203 East Cary Street, Box 26511, Richmond, VA 23261. (804) 644-4654. Uses a child sponsorship program to raise money to help children and families around the world.

Church World Service, Box 968, Elkhart, IN 46515. (219) 264-3102. Distributes emergency and development aid around the world. The relief arm of the National Council of Churches in Christ.

Compassion International, 3955 Cragwood Drive, Box 7000, Colorado Springs, CO 80933. (719) 594-9900. Runs a Christian child development program that provides funds for education, nutrition, training and Bible study around the world.

Habitat for Humanity International, Inc., 419 West Church Street, Americus, GA 31709, (912) 924-6935. Builds and rehabilitates homes for low-income people around the world.

Heifer Project International, International Learning and Livestock Center, Route 2, Box 33, Perryville, AR 72126, (501) 889-5124. An international development organization that raises and gives high-quality livestock to low-income farmers around the world.

Oxfam America, 115 Broadway, Boston, MA 02116. (617) 482-1211. An international agency that funds self-help development and disaster relief projects in developing countries.

World Vision, Special Programs, 919 West Huntington Drive, Monrovia, CA 91016. 1-800-444-2522. An interdenominational, evangelical organization that provides emergency and development aid around the world.

CLOSING: I Can Make a Difference

What You'll Need

- Different-color construction paper (one sheet per person)
- Markers (at least one per person)
- Cellophane tape
- An offering plate or basket
- Tables and chairs

Time Needed:

10 minutes

Everyone can help people in need. In this closing, group members will make a commitment to reach out and minister to people who are less fortunate.

How to Prepare

1. Gather the supplies listed in the "What You'll Need" box. You can use the same offering plate or basket used in the "Sharing Charades" activity.

2. Read the "How to Lead" section to be sure you understand the activity.

3. Practice what you're going to say to the group. It doesn't need to be word for word; say it in your own words so it will be more meaningful to your group.

4. Choose an appropriate song to sing as a group to close the meeting.

How to Lead

1. After the learning time, give each person a piece of construction paper and a colored marker. Ask group members to sit around tables where they can concentrate and write.

2. When everyone is ready, say: Sometimes it's easy to think, "I can't really do anything to help people who are hungry." But each of us *can* help in some way. We can help as a group through a missions project. And we can help as individuals.

Think about the eating utensil you were given at the beginning of the meeting. It's hard to eat a meal with just one of them. Try eating soup with a fork or steak with a spoon. In the same way, each of us has something important and unique to contribute to help people in need.

3. Then ask group members each to write on their construction paper one thing they commit themselves to do to help people in need. Tell them *not* to write their names on their papers. They could write, for example, "I will donate $5 per month from my paycheck to hunger relief organizations" or "I will volunteer once a month to serve in a soup kitchen." Encourage group members each to write something they are actually willing to do. Be sure you write something yourself. Allow about five minutes.

4. As group members write, go around the room and give them each a piece of tape to attach their utensil to their paper.

5. Form a circle when everyone is ready. Place the food basket full of donated food in the center of the circle. Then say: As I pass around the offering plate (or basket), put your commitment into it. Think about what you have just challenged yourself to do for others.

6. After the offering plate has gone around the circle, say, I'd like to pass the offering plate again. Take out someone else's card and read it to the group. Then place the written commitment in the food basket as our commitment as a group to help others in need.

7. Close by joining hands, right arm over left, linked together in one united circle as a group dedicated to keeping the commitments each individual has made. Sing a song together and close with prayer.

Playing the Dating Game

Dating should be a time to get to know people and have fun. Yet dating can be filled with fears and pressures that take away from the focus on building relationships. This meeting encourages group members to think about how they act toward others when dating, and it explores Christian attitudes toward dating.

Objectives

In this meeting, group members will:
- have fun talking about the "perfect date";
- ask and discuss some of their questions about dating;
- discover dating guidelines based on scripture; and
- affirm personal qualities in each other.

Biblical Foundation

The Bible offers guidelines for Christian living that say a lot about dating. This meeting will explore the following passages: Romans 12:1-18; Galatians 5:16-26 and 6:1-10; 1 Corinthians 6:12-20; 1 Thessalonians 4:1-12; and James 1:1-27 and 2:1-18.

Adult Leader's Responsibilities

1. Meet with the meeting coordinator two weeks ahead of time. Help the meeting coordinator find people to lead each aspect of the meeting.

2. Call meeting leaders four or five days in advance to ask if they have any questions and to be sure they have gathered all supplies and have prepared adequately.

Meeting Coordinator's Responsibilities

1. Make a photocopy of the instructions of each part of the meeting to give to the leaders.

2. At least two weeks before the meeting, find group members to lead different aspects of the meeting. (If you wish, you may lead one of the sections yourself.) Give leaders each a photocopy of the meeting element they're leading. Encourage leaders to find helpers if needed.

3. Schedule a planning session one week before the event with all leaders to go through the meeting to be sure they understand it.

4. Find someone to coordinate refreshments to serve after the meeting. Suggest serving punch and inexpensive hors d'oeuvres to imitate what would be served at a prom.

5. The day before the meeting, call all the leaders to make sure they're ready for the meeting. Go over the activity with each leader to make sure he or she has not forgotten any details.

Meeting Outline				
Coordinator: _____				
Activity	Estimated Time	Who's Responsible	Telephone	Confirmed
Community-Builder: WCGN News Report	15 minutes			
Learning Time: Dating Dilemmas	20 minutes			
Bible Study: Sharing Your Feelings	15 minutes			
Closing: Prom Night	10 minutes			
Refreshments				

WCGN News Report

What You'll Need

- ☐ Supplies to make a cardboard TV camera (shoe box, scissors, mailing paper, construction paper, tape, markers)
- ☐ Supplies to make a paper microphone (construction paper, cotton, string)
- ☐ Paper and pencils
- ☐ Interview questions on note cards
- ☐ Optional: video camera, VCR and television
- ☐ Chairs

Time Needed:

15 minutes

"I get so nervous when I go out on a date. I never know what to expect. Everyone is so different."

"I don't think dating should be so scary. I think there should be a way to go out on a date and just have fun without having to always worry about what the other person thinks of you."

You and your friends have probably shared similar conversations. This community-builder lets you imagine the perfect date.

 How to Prepare

1. Gather the supplies listed in the "What You'll Need" box.

2. Read the "How to Lead" section to be sure you understand the activity. Practice being a TV news reporter.

3. Make a paper microphone by cutting out a triangle from construction paper and taping it together like an ice cream cone. Stuff cotton in the top and tape string to the bottom. (See Sample 4-1.)

4. Make a TV camera out of a medium-size box (such as a shoe box) covered with brown mailing paper. Cut a hole to look through, and attach a round construction paper lens on the front. Write "WCGN News" on the camera's side. (See Sample 4-1.)

5. Prepare interview questions that will help everyone have fun and think at the same time. Write the questions on note cards so you can carry them easily when "interviewing" people for your TV show. Here are some suggestions:

- Why do you date? What's fun about it?
- How do you decide who to ask out for a date? What characteristics would you want the person to have?
- Do you think dating is a good way to get to know someone? What's a better way to get to know a person of the opposite sex?
- What do you do if you don't want to go on a date with someone? Do you think it's important to tell that person the truth? Why or why not?
- Have you ever felt hurt because someone wouldn't ask you out? What did you do about it?
- How does it feel when someone turns you down for a date?
- Do you like to date a lot of different people or just one person? Explain your answer.
- Should both girls and guys ask people out? Why or why not?
- Who should pay on a date? the guy? the person who asks for the date? both people? Explain your answer.
- How late should you stay out on a date? Should parents have any say about when you get home? Why or why not?

If you have a large group, you may want to ask some questions twice. Reporters sometimes do this by saying: "And how about you. What do you think?"

6. Ask two or three friends to be your "camera crew" for the interviews.

7. Before the meeting, hide your camera, microphone and interview question cards near the meeting room door. Also arrange the chairs in a circle so it will be easier to interview.

8. Optional approach: If equipment is available, you could also videotape the interviews. Then play back the interviews during the refreshment time.

How to Lead

1. When it's time to begin the meeting, give each person a piece of paper and a pencil. Begin by saying: Suppose you could have your ultimate "dream date." You could go anywhere and do anything. Your companion would be perfect. What would that date be like?

Now write an ad for the "personals" column to help you find that perfect person for that perfect date. Your ad should include:

● where you would go;

● a description of the person you want to go with; and

● how you would expect that perfect person to act during your date.

2. Allow group members about five minutes to write their ads. As they're finishing, you and your "camera crew" can slip out of the room to prepare for the interviews.

3. When you're ready, come into the room with your "camera crew" close behind. Introduce yourself to the group by saying: Hi, everyone. I'm _____ _____ (your name) _____, a reporter for the World Christian Good News (WCGN) Evening News. I'm reporting live tonight from the _____ _____ (your youth group's name) _____ meeting to find out what makes a perfect date.

4. Then begin asking group members interview questions. Ham it up and have fun. Ask follow-up questions to find out more about why group members answered the way they did. Keep the pace lively, but do give them a chance to answer. If someone can't think of an answer when you ask, just say to the next person, "While she's thinking, let me ask you" . . . and ask the next question. Make sure you interview everybody at the meeting.

5. When you've interviewed everyone, turn to the camera and say: There you have it, folks. That's what people want in a date. From _____ (your church name) _____, this is _____ (your name) _____ reporting live for WCGN. Back to Andrea and Tyrone in the studios.

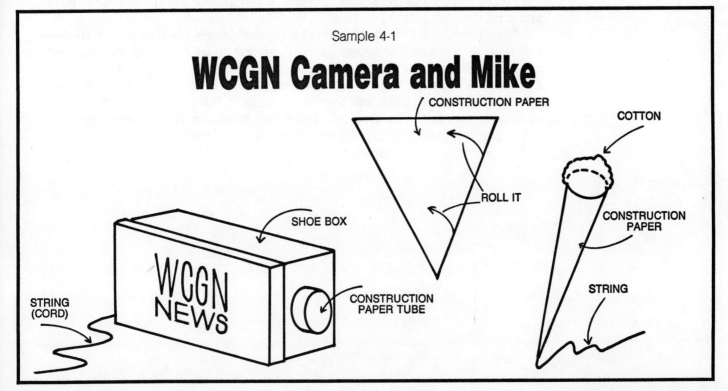

Sample 4-1

WCGN Camera and Mike

CONSTRUCTION PAPER

COTTON

ROLL IT

SHOE BOX

CONSTRUCTION PAPER

CONSTRUCTION PAPER TUBE

STRING (CORD)

WCGN NEWS

STRING

Dating Dilemmas

What You'll Need

☐ Paper and pencils
☐ Tables and chairs

Time Needed:

20 minutes

"I don't have anyone to talk to. I can't tell my parents. They'll just yell at me. I'm afraid to tell my friends because I don't want to be the subject of next week's gossip around school."

Sometimes we feel like we have no one to talk to. This activity gives you and your friends an opportunity to talk about the fears and problems you have on dates.

How to Prepare

1. Gather the supplies listed in the "What You'll Need" box.

2. Read the "How to Lead" section to be sure you understand the activity. Practice your introduction to the activity.

How to Lead

1. When the TV reporter "signs off," ask group members to sit at the tables. Give everyone a sheet of paper and a pencil.

2. Introduce the exercise by saying: Imagine for a minute that a world-famous dating expert writes a question-and-answer column about dating for our youth group newsletter. It's called "Dating Dilemmas." What questions would you want this column to answer?

3. Then have group members each write a brief letter to "Dating Dilemmas," asking a question or telling about a problem or concern. They can ask for advice on any subject—physical involvement on dates, drugs and alcohol on dates, how to get up the courage to ask someone out, or parents' attitudes toward dating. Tell group members to keep their letters anonymous and not to use any names. Allow about five minutes.

4. When group members have finished writing, collect and shuffle the papers.

5. Next, form teams of five people each. Try to include a good balance of guys and girls on each team.

6. Then give each team five "Dating Dilemmas" letters. Have each team choose one letter to answer. Encourage group members to be open and honest, and emphasize that no one should make fun of anyone else's question. Allow about five minutes for each team to agree on an answer to its problem or concern.

7. Finally, bring all the teams together in a circle. Have a group member from each team read both the letter and the team's response. If you have time, give other group members a chance to respond to the letter.

BIBLE STUDY: # Sharing Your Feelings

What You'll Need

☐ Bibles
☐ Pencils
☐ Four tables and chairs
☐ Copies of "Sharing Your Feelings" (Handout 4-2)
☐ Newsprint and markers

Time Needed:

15 minutes

Many of the New Testament books were actually letters written to friends and early churches, giving advice on how they should and should not act. In this Bible study, you and your friends have a chance to share your feelings about dating and to explore the Christian standards for life set by the early Christians. You'll also write a dating guideline based on Bible passages.

How to Prepare

1. Gather the supplies listed in the "What You'll Need" box.
2. Read the "How to Lead" section to be sure you understand the activity.
3. Make a copy of "Sharing Your Feelings" (Handout 4-2) for each group member.

How to Lead

1. After the "Dating Dilemmas" discussion, divide the group into four teams.
2. Give everyone a pencil and a copy of the "Sharing Your Feelings" handout (Handout 4-2). Assign each team one set of questions to answer. Then have group members individually complete the open-ended statements under #1 in their team's section.
3. Next, have each team read the Bible passage together and write a dating guideline based on the passage.
4. When all teams have finished, invite group members to sit in a circle and tell about their guidelines. Write the guidelines on newsprint so they'll be easier to talk about. Give the group time to talk about the guidelines. To get discussion going, ask questions such as:
  ● Is this guideline fair? Why or why not?
  ● Do you think this guideline is what God wants from us? Why or why not?
  ● Is it hard to follow this guideline as a teenager today? Why or why not?
  ● Can you think of a more appropriate guideline for Christian teenagers? What would it be?

Sharing Your Feelings

This is your chance to make the rules! Each team will write a dating guideline based on a Bible passage. First, each person answers the open-ended statements in #1. Then, together as a team, read the Bible passage specified in #2, and write a dating guideline that you believe would apply to all Christian teenagers.

Team 1

1. Complete these statements by yourself:

   The greatest thing about dating is. . .

   I think dating should be . . .

2. As a team, read Romans 12:1-18.

3. Write a dating guideline about how we should use the gifts that God has given us.

Team 2

1. Complete these statements by yourself:

   I'm old enough to . . .

   When I go out on a date, I expect . . .

2. As a team, read Galatians 5:16-26 and 6:1-10.

3. Write a dating guideline about how God wants us to treat other people.

Team 3

1. Complete these statements by yourself:

   I don't like it when . . .

   I feel rejected when . . .

2. As a team, read 1 Corinthians 6:12-20.

3. Write a dating guideline about any limits we should place on ourselves as Christians. These can concern both what we do and how we act on dates.

Team 4

1. Complete these statements by yourself:

   I show I care by . . .

   I'm responsible for . . .

2. As a team, read 1 Thessalonians 4:1-12 and James 1:1-27 and 2:1-18.

3. Write a dating guideline about whether we're responsible for how we act on a date.

CLOSING: # Prom Night

What You'll Need

☐ Paper boutonnieres or corsages
☐ Note cards and pencils
☐ A circle of chairs
☐ A small table
☐ Straight pins

Time Needed:

10 minutes

Often when we want a date, we look for someone who's the most attractive or popular. In this activity, we'll look past these superficial qualities and think about each person's positive personality traits.

How to Prepare

1. Gather the supplies listed in the "What You'll Need" box.

2. Read the "How to Lead" section to be sure you understand the activity.

3. Make a paper boutonniere or corsage for everyone in the group. These can be as simple as daisies cut out of construction paper. Or you can make tissue-paper carnations.

4. Choose a song about love or friendship to sing at the end. If possible, ask a guitarist or pianist to accompany the singing.

How to Lead

1. When you've finished the Bible study, stay in a circle and give each group member a card and a pencil. Spread the flowers on a small table in the center of the circle.

2. Have group members each match up with the person directly opposite them in the circle. Then say: Let's pretend that someone asked you to recommend your partner across the room for a date. You know that person would be a great date—not for the usual reasons such as good looks, popularity, good grades or money, but for his or her personal characteristics—kindness, sensitivity, thoughtfulness and so on.

Think of one positive reason why your partner across the circle would make a perfect date for the prom. Focus on inner, personal qualities, not outward things. When you think of a reason, write it on your card. Then pick an appropriate flower to give to the person as you read your card. Remember, your comments should be completely positive.

3. To help group members understand, give an example yourself. You might say: Sandra is my partner. I could write, "Sandra would be a perfect prom date for you because she's the most compassionate person I know."

4. Give group members time to write, then have each of them volunteer to read their trait aloud and give the card and a flower to their partner. Let group members each pin on their own flower to wear home as a reminder of their inner beauty.

5. Close the meeting with a song about love or friendship and with a prayer, thanking God for the many gifts he has given each person and for making each person unique and special.

6. Serve refreshments immediately after the meeting. If you videotaped the interviews during the community-builder, play them back for the whole group.

I Hear Music

The average teenager listens to music almost three hours every day. That's 20 hours and 30 minutes each week, 82 hours each month and 1,066 hours each year.

If young people listen to that much music, it's important to know what that music is saying. And it's important to make wise choices when selecting music. This meeting examines rock music's influence on young people. It encourages people to look for music that is both enjoyable and worthwhile.

Objectives

In this meeting, group members will:
● listen to various kinds of music to discover what they like and don't like;
● analyze popular lyrics and album covers; and
● think about how their faith should influence their music choices.

Biblical Foundation

The music we listen to often reflects the life we live. This Bible study helps people examine music choices based on how we should live our daily lives. It examines Luke 16:1-12; Colossians 3:8-17; and Psalm 96:1.

Adult Leader's Responsibilities

1. Meet with the meeting coordinator at least three weeks ahead of time. Help the coordinator find people to lead the meeting. Also decide whether to meet at the church or in someone's home (which may be easier, since you'll need access to a stereo).

2. Call leaders several days in advance to ask if they have any questions and to be sure they have gathered all supplies and have prepared adequately. Be sure the meeting has been announced and publicized. Remind group members each to bring a favorite record to the meeting.

3. Call again the night before the meeting to double-check that the leaders are all set. Go over the checklists to make sure they haven't forgotten anything.

Meeting Coordinator's Responsibilities

1. Make a photocopy of the instructions for each part of the meeting to give to the leaders.

2. Meet with the adult leader to decide where to hold the meeting. You'll need a place that has a stereo.

3. If you decide to have the meeting in a home, find a family that would be willing to host the meeting. Tell the parents what the meeting will be about, what you'll need and how many people you expect to attend.

4. At least three weeks before the meeting, find group members to lead different aspects of the meeting. (If you wish, you may lead one of the sections yourself.) Give leaders each a photocopy of the meeting element they're leading. Encourage leaders to find helpers if needed.

5. Two weeks before the event, schedule a planning session with all leaders to go through the meeting and be sure everyone understands it.

6. Find someone to coordinate refreshments for after the meeting.

7. Announce and publicize the meeting two weeks in advance. Ask group members each to bring their favorite album to the meeting.

8. The day before the meeting, call all the leaders to make sure they're ready for the meeting.

Meeting Outline				
Coordinator: _____				
Activity	Estimated Time	Who's Responsible	Telephone	Confirmed
Community-Builder: Critic's Choice	20 minutes			
Learning Time: For Your Eyes Only	10 minutes			
Bible Study: Music With a Message	15 minutes			
Closing: The Record Hop	10 minutes			
Refreshments				

Critic's Choice

What You'll Need

☐ Stereo equipment (turntable, tape player or compact disc player)
☐ Albums
☐ Background music

Time Needed:

20 minutes

Have you ever heard a disc jockey play short excerpts from songs so people can call in to guess the song or singer? This activity is a variation on those popular call-in shows. Your group will have fun thinking about all the different kinds of music people listen to.

 ## How to Prepare

1. Read the "How to Lead" section to be sure you understand the activity.
2. Gather the supplies listed in the "What You'll Need" box.
3. Pick songs to excerpt for the game. You'll need a song for every two people at the meeting. For example, if 20 people usually attend, pick out 10 songs—or 12 to be safe. Choose a wide variety—rock, jazz, soul, country, contemporary Christian, folk, classical, oldies and new releases. If you don't have a wide selection yourself, ask friends, parents or your youth minister for suggestions. Or your public library may have albums you can check out.
4. Organize the albums in the order you want to play them. Note which song on each album you'll excerpt. Read the album cover to find out a little about the song. Take some notes about the artist, title, when the song was released, whether it was a hit and so forth, so you can tell the group about the song.
5. Select an appropriate album to play as background music as group members arrive for the meeting.

 ## How to Lead

1. As the first group members arrive, start the background music.
2. When it's time to start the meeting, have group members each pick a partner who likes a *different* kind of music than they do. For example, someone who likes rock music might find a partner who likes jazz. If there's an extra person, have one team of three. Give teams each a number so they'll know which song they're evaluating.
3. When everyone is settled, explain the game (mimic a disc jockey if you want to): Hello all you music fans. Welcome to "Critic's Choice," the hottest game show in _____(your town)_____. Tonight we have some great music and some great competitors. So if we're all ready, let's get started.

Here's how it works: I'll play a short excerpt from a record for each team. Based on that excerpt, the team must decide whether to give the song a "thumbs up" or "thumbs down."

Is everybody ready? Here's song #1!

4. Play a 30-second excerpt from the first song. Don't say anything about the song's title, artist or when it came out. Ask the team for its evaluation. Then ask what team members based their decision on—music? beat? lyrics? voice? message? style?
5. When the first team has evaluated its song, quickly tell the group about the song, using the notes you took from the album cover.
6. Then move on to the other songs. Announce each one so teams will know it's their turn.
7. After all the teams have played, ask group members whether or not they would buy a particular album based on their evaluations of these excerpts.

For Your Eyes Only

What You'll Need

☐ Copies of "Album Evaluation Hand-out" (Handout 5-1)
☐ Pencils
☐ Albums and lyrics brought by group members
☐ Extra albums and lyrics

Time Needed:

10 minutes

How many times do we really listen to the words and think about the meaning of the songs we hear? What are our favorite songs saying? In this activity, your group will take a few minutes to think about what popular songs are really saying.

 ## How to Prepare

1. Read the "How to Lead" section to be sure you understand the activity.
2. Gather the supplies listed in the "What You'll Need" box.
3. The week before the meeting, ask group members each to bring their favorite album to the next meeting. Ask them to write out the words to their favorite song on the album. Also put an announcement in the newsletter. Tell group members whether to bring records, tapes or compact discs, depending on the equipment you have available. Remind them to label their albums so they won't get mixed up.
4. Collect a few extra albums with lyrics written out, in case someone doesn't bring one to the meeting.

 ## How to Lead

1. After the "Critic's Choice" activity, ask group members each to get the album they brought. Then divide the group into five teams. Don't spend a lot of time dividing them into teams; just count off: one, two, three, four, five. Have each team form a circle in a different area of the room.
2. Make sure group members each have labeled their album and have written out the words to their favorite song. If any group members didn't bring albums and words, let them choose from the extras you brought.
3. Then have each team trade albums with another team so no one has his or her own album.
4. Have each team pick one song from the five albums that it likes best.
5. Distribute the pencils and the "Album Evaluation Handout" (one per team). Ask each team to evaluate the album cover and the lyrics, using the questions on the handout. Allow about five minutes.
6. When teams have finished, bring the whole group back together. Have each team report on its evaluation.

Album Evaluation Handout

Answer the following questions about the album cover you chose:

1. What do the pictures suggest?

2. What do the pictures make you think of?

3. How do you feel when you look at this album cover (ashamed, happy, excited, peaceful)?

4. What do you think the album designers were trying to communicate?

5. Do you like the album cover? Why or why not?

Answer the following questions about the song you chose:

1. What do the song's words make you think of?

2. What is the songwriter trying to say?

3. Do the words in this song mean the same thing to everyone? Why or why not?

4. Do you think the song has any hidden meanings? Why or why not?

5. Does this song mention topics such as sex, drugs, alcohol or profanity? How do these references make you feel?

6. How does this song make you feel?

7. Does the song say something of value? Do you think all songs should express values? Why or why not?

BIBLE STUDY: **Music With a Message**

What You'll Need

☐ A song that reflects the Bible study themes
☐ Bibles
☐ Pencils
☐ Copies of "Songs From Scripture" (Handout 5-2)
☐ Three tables and chairs

Time Needed:

15 minutes

Many songs we listen to deal with everyday problems and troubles. They often present ideas about how we should live our lives. Some of the suggestions are good; some aren't.

This Bible study shows how songs can reflect Christian principles. It gives your group a chance to write songs based on scripture.

 ## How to Prepare

1. Read the "How to Lead" section to be sure you understand the activity.
2. Gather the supplies listed in the "What You'll Need" box.
3. Find a song about one of the themes in the Bible study (practicing Christian principles in everyday life, using money wisely and being honest and trustworthy). The song can be by a Christian recording artist or a popular group with a positive message. If you need help, ask other group members or your youth minister for ideas.

 ## How to Lead

1. After the album, cover and lyrics evaluation, divide the group into three different teams. Have each team sit around a table.
2. Give each person a Bible, a pencil and a copy of Handout 5-2, "Songs From Scripture."
3. Ask each team to read Luke 16:1-12, Colossians 3:8-17 and Psalm 96:1.
4. Then assign each team a section of the "Songs From Scripture" handout. Ask each group to write a simple song to explain its verses. The song can be based on a popular tune or a nursery rhyme. Allow about five minutes for teams to write their songs.
5. When all the teams are ready, have them each read or sing the song they wrote.
6. After all three teams have read or sung, read Colossians 3:8-17 aloud. Ask:
● Does this passage apply to the music we listen to? Why or why not?
● How do you think the music we listen to should reflect our faith?
● Is it okay for Christians to listen to any kind of music? If not, what kinds should we avoid?
● What are some songs you listen to that you believe reflect Christian values? Explain.
Allow several minutes for discussion.
7. Conclude the Bible study by playing the song you found which has a theme that fits the Bible study.

Songs From Scripture

1. Luke 16:8

This verse challenges us to apply Christian principles in our daily lives with the same enthusiasm we have for other things we do, such as playing sports, collecting records, buying clothes or socializing. Imagine what changes we could make in the world and in our own neighborhood, family and school if we worked hard at living a Christian life.

Write a song that encourages Christians to live what they believe.

2. Luke 16:9

In this verse we learn that we're to use money for what we need and to help the less fortunate. We aren't asked to throw away money and expect others to take care of us. Nor should we be controlled by our desire for money.

Write a song that challenges Christians to take their financial responsibilities seriously.

3. Luke 16:10-12

God holds us responsible for how we use our time. We need to realize that many little things in life are just as important as the seemingly bigger issues. For example, being kind to people may seem insignificant, but it's so important.

Write a song that challenges Christians to use their time wisely.

The Record Hop

What You'll Need

- [ ] Black and white construction paper
- [ ] Pens or pencils
- [ ] Stopwatch or other timer
- [ ] Scissors
- [ ] Glue
- [ ] Tables and chairs

Time Needed:

10 minutes

Do you ever get tired of others criticizing the music you listen to? During this closing, you'll have a chance to tell everything good about your favorite songs.

How to Prepare

1. Read the "How to Lead" section to be sure you understand the activity.

2. Gather the supplies listed in the "What You'll Need" box.

3. Make a paper record for each person in your group by cutting a large circle out of black paper. Then cut a smaller circle out of white paper, and glue it in the center of the black paper, like a label on a record. The white circle needs to be big enough that your whole group can write on it. If your group is large, glue a white circle to each side for more space.

4. On each record label, write a different question about music people listen to. Think of your own questions, or include questions like the following:

- When you first hear a new song, what's the first thing you listen for? the singer's name? the words? the music? something else?
- What makes a song your favorite?
- What's your favorite subject for a song to be about?
- What kind of music do you like most (rock, jazz, country, classical and so forth)? Why?
- Is it okay if you like different music from your friends? Why or why not?
- Will you listen to a song on the radio even if you don't like it? Or do you change the station? Explain.
- Do you have to like all the songs on an album before you buy it? If not, how many do you have to like?
- Does a singer's lifestyle influence whether you like his or her music? If so, what attracts you and what detracts you?
- Name a song that shares a good message.
- Name a song that makes you feel happy and good about yourself.

5. Choose a song to sing as a closing prayer. The Lord's Prayer is one example. Check your church hymnal or youth songbook for other possibilities. If possible, find a pianist or guitarist to accompany the singing.

How to Lead

1. After the Bible study, gather the group around a table with each person sitting directly across from a partner. Put a paper record on the table in front of each person. If you have an extra person, have one person sit at the head of the table to keep time. Everyone will get a chance to keep time as you rotate around the table.

2. Explain the activity. Group members each ask their partner the question on the record in front of them. They each have to write on the record their partner's answer before time is called in about 15 seconds. Then group members each move quickly to the next chair so they have a new partner and a new question.

3. When everyone understands the activity, begin. Keep the pace lively so group members barely have time to sit down, read the question and write the answer.

4. When everyone has gone around the table, ask group members each to read the question and responses on the record in front of them.

5. Close the meeting by singing the prayer you chose.

The Two Sides of Peer Pressure

Friends are important. They give us companionship. They affirm us. They help us sort out our questions and decisions. But friends can also pressure us to do things we wouldn't otherwise do.

This meeting helps group members see the influence—both positive and negative—their friends have on them. The activities help young people examine the unique contributions they can make to a group, and they challenge teenagers to support each other.

Objectives

In this meeting, group members will:
- see how each individual contributes to a group;
- discover ways they feel pressure to do what the group wants them to do;
- discover how people in the Bible dealt with peer pressures they faced, and
- find ways they can support each other.

Biblical Foundation

We often don't think about how people in the Bible interacted in groups. The Bible study looks at some of these people and the choices they had to make. The meeting emphasizes that we all comfort each other because God comforts us (2 Corinthians 1:3-4).

Adult Leader's Responsibilities

1. Meet with the meeting coordinator at least two weeks in advance. Help the coordinator find group members to lead each aspect of the meeting. Have the coordinator arrange a meeting with the meeting leaders two weeks before the meeting.

2. Call all leaders to make sure they get their materials ready before the meeting. Go over the checklist with each leader.

Meeting Coordinator's Responsibilities

1. Photocopy the instructions for each part of the meeting to give to the leaders.

2. At least two weeks before the meeting, meet with your adult leader to find group members to be in charge of every aspect of peer meeting. (If you wish, you may lead one of the sections yourself.) Encourage leaders to find helpers if they need them.

3. Schedule a planning session one week before the meeting to be sure the leaders understand their parts in the meeting.

4. Find someone to coordinate refreshments.

5. The day before the meeting, call all the leaders to make sure they're ready.

Meeting Outline

Coordinator: _____

Activity	Estimated Time	Who's Responsible	Telephone	Confirmed
Community-Builder: Balloon Beasts	15 minutes			
Learning Time: Every Piece Counts	15 minutes			
Bible Study: Leaders and Followers	20 minutes			
Affirmation: The Acceptance Game	5 minutes			
Closing: Life Saver	5 minutes			
Refreshments				

Balloon Beasts

What You'll Need

☐ Animal balloons or long balloons
☐ Three boxes of animal-shape crackers or candies
☐ Craft supplies (markers, glue, scissors, construction paper)
☐ Table

Time Needed:

15 minutes

Have you ever seen a clown make animals out of balloons? The animals the clown makes seem similar to each other, yet each one is different from the others.

This activity uses animal balloons to emphasize that, while we're all the same, we're all different too. Making balloon animals together will prepare your group for a meeting of fun and teamwork.

How to Prepare

1. Gather the supplies listed in the "What You'll Need" box.

2. Read the "How to Lead" section to be sure you understand the activity.

3. Buy several bags of animal balloons (available from party supply stores). You'll need at least one balloon per person in your group—plus some extras for practice and in case some pop. Make sure you have at least seven different colors of balloons. (If your group has fewer than 12 or 15 members, you'll need at least three different colors.)

4. Divide the balloons into different colors. Then make bundles that include one balloon of each color. Hold the balloons together with a rubber band. (This way you can give out balloons one set at a time to keep from having too many people with the same color of balloon.)

5. Practice making balloon animals so you can demonstrate making them. (Instructions are printed on the package.)

6. Get three different kinds of animal-shape crackers or candies for prizes.

7. Blow up some extra balloons before the meeting for your demonstration and as replacements for popped balloons.

How to Lead

1. Give group members each a balloon as they arrive for the meeting. (Give out balloons from one set at a time so you don't have too many people with the same color.) Ask group members each to blow up and tie their balloon. Encourage them not to pop the balloons since they'll need them for a contest.

2. When all the balloons are blown up, have group members each team up with six other people who have different-color balloons. (Every team should have seven people with seven different-color balloons.) If you have extra people, have eight on some teams, or form a smaller team. If your group is small, form three-person teams, and give each group member two balloons.

3. After all the teams are organized, demonstrate how to make a simple balloon animal. Then say: It's time for you to make your balloons come to life. You have five minutes to make a balloon animal using all seven of your team's balloons. It doesn't matter what kind of animal it is—you can even make one up. Just remember, we'll give prizes for the following:

● most creative animal;
● easiest animal to identify; and
● best use of balloons.

Your team can decorate your animal using the craft supplies on the table to make eyelashes, a mouth or whatever else you want.

Everybody ready? Go!

4. Give the teams five minutes to make their animals.

5. Select someone from each team to form a panel of judges. Have the judges pick a winner in each category. As you enthusiastically announce the winners, give the winners the animal-cracker prizes to share with the whole group.

Every Piece Counts

What You'll Need

- ☐ A letter-size envelope for each person
- ☐ Construction sets (such as Lego or Tinkertoys)
- ☐ Markers
- ☐ Tables

Time Needed:

15 minutes

It's always harder for groups to make decisions than for one person to make them. Groups have to consider each person's ideas and then work out a compromise. When you're working alone, you don't have to check with anyone. But group decision-making can also have its advantages. This activity focuses on the contribution that each person makes to a group.

 ## How to Prepare

1. Gather the supplies listed in the "What You'll Need" box. You may be able to borrow construction sets from a children's Sunday school classroom. A set with a lot of different-shape pieces is best.

2. Read the "How to Lead" section to be sure you understand the activity.

3. Divide the envelopes into stacks of five. If, for example, 30 people usually come to meetings, you'll have six stacks of five envelopes. Choose a color for each stack, and write the color on the envelopes using the appropriate marker.

4. Put five construction-set pieces into each envelope. Try to vary the types of pieces you put in each color group.

5. Seal the envelopes and arrange them by color—a red, followed by a green, a blue, a yellow and so on, depending on the colors you use.

 ## How to Lead

1. After the community-builder, give everyone a color-coded envelope. Then have group members find the other four people with the same-color envelope. Ask each five-person team to find open workspace at a table or on the floor.

2. Then say to the group: Inside your envelopes are pieces from a construction set. Your team must decide on a structure you'd like to build, using all the pieces. But you must each decide how to use the five pieces in your own envelope. No one else can tell you where to put your pieces.

3. Answer any questions teams have about the activity. Then let them start building. Allow about 10 minutes.

4. When the teams are finished, bring them together into a large circle. Have a group member from each team describe the team's structure and how the team decided what to make.

5. Then ask specific questions about the building process:

● Did anyone feel pressured to build what other team members wanted to build? Or did people feel free to build what they wanted? Explain.

● Did anyone feel frustrated because someone on the team wanted to use his or her pieces in a different way? How did you resolve that tension?

● How did this exercise remind you of any other areas of life where you feel pressure to conform to what other people want? Be specific.

● Who puts the most pressure on you to conform to group standards? friends? parents? yourself? Give examples.

● How do you decide when to cooperate with a group and when to do things your own way? Give examples.

● What are some ways you've learned to respond to this pressure?

6. After the discussion, thank group members for sharing their insights.

BIBLE STUDY: Leaders and Followers

What You'll Need

- A copy of Handout 6-1 for every five participants
- Bibles—several translations
- Pencils
- Newsprint and markers

Time Needed:

20 minutes

Sample 6-2

Key to "Leaders and Followers" Puzzle

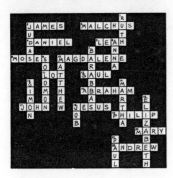

Do you sometimes feel that you're being asked to say no when everyone else is saying yes? Many people in the Bible felt the same. This Bible study focuses on people who made tough choices in biblical times.

How to Prepare

1. Gather the supplies listed in the "What You'll Need" box. Make enough copies of Handout 6-1, "Leaders and Followers," for each team of five group members. And have several Bible translations on hand for teams to use when solving the puzzle.

2. Read the "How to Lead" section to be sure you understand the activity.

3. Prepare newsprint charts for the discussion time. Put each of the following labels at the top of a separate sheet of newsprint: "Members of a Group," "Influential Leaders," "People Who Made Tough Choices."

How to Lead

1. After the learning time discussion, have group members get back into their teams of five. Give each team pencils and a copy of Handout 6-1. Give a Bible to anyone who didn't bring one.

2. Tell teams each to solve the puzzle together. Ask teams to look for people who were strong leaders, people who were followers and people who made tough decisions. Allow about 10 minutes.

3. When everyone has finished the puzzle, bring teams together to form a circle. Go through the puzzle, reading the questions and letting teams supply the answers. Check the answers against the key in Sample 6-2.

4. Post the three sheets of newsprint. Then lead the group in a discussion of the people mentioned in the crossword puzzle. Begin by asking group members to put each person in the puzzle into one of the following categories:

- Members of a group
- Influential leaders
- People who made tough choices

As group members make suggestions, ask them to explain their reasoning. Then write each name on the appropriate sheet of newsprint.

5. Then ask some general questions about the people in the puzzle:

- What kind of group leader was Jesus?
- What did he ask his group members to do?
- What other characteristics do you see in the other leaders?
- How are these leaders like strong leaders today? Explain.
- What are some similarities between the tough choices people made in the Bible and tough choices we have to make today?
- What do the ways people in the Bible responded to pressures tell us about how we can respond to pressures we feel? Give examples.

Leaders and Followers

Across

2. John's brother. (Matthew 4:21 and 10:2)
3. Peter cut off this person's ear when Jesus was arrested in the Garden of Gethsemane. (John 18:10)
4. A dream interpreter. (Daniel 2:24-30)
5. Jacob's first wife. (Genesis 29:16-30 and 33:7)
8. A great leader and lawgiver. (Exodus 2:1-10 and Deuteronomy 34:1)
10. The first person to see Jesus after the Resurrection. (Matthew 27:55-56, 61)
11. Abraham's nephew who chose to live in Sodom. (Genesis 11:31; 13:12; and 14:16)
12. Israel's first king. (1 Samuel 9:15-21 and 10:20-24)
15. The person considered to be the father of Israel. (Genesis 25:7-8)
17. The forerunner to the Messiah. (Luke 1:5-25; 3:1-20; and 7:18-20)
18. He told the parable of the mustard seed. (Matthew 13:31-32)
19. A disciple who was also an early church official. (Matthew 10:3 and Acts 8:4-8)
20. Jesus' mother. (Luke 1:26-38 and 2:1-7)
22. Peter's brother and one of the disciples. (Matthew 4:18 and John 1:40)

Down

1. King David's great-grandmother. (Ruth 4:13-22)
2. The person who betrayed Jesus. (Matthew 10:4; 26:14-16; and 27:3)
6. A woman who lived and taught in the temple. (Luke 2:36-38)
7. The prisoner Pilate released instead of Jesus. (Matthew 27:15-18)
9. A writer and collector of wise sayings. (2 Samuel 12:24; 1 Kings 1:11-14; and 1 Kings 3:15-28)
10. The disciple who was originally a tax collector. (Matthew 9:9 and 10:3)
13. The person in whose house Jesus was anointed. (Mark 14:3)
14. Her brother's name was Lazarus and her sister's name was Mary. (Luke 10:38-42)
16. John the Baptist's mother. (Luke 1:39-42)
18. Central figure of an Old Testament book that explores the problem of suffering. (Job 1:1-5)
21. An early persecutor of Christians who later became a great missionary and church leader. (Acts 7:54-8:1a and 19:8-12)

The Acceptance Game

What You'll Need

☐ An open space

Time Needed:

5 minutes

We often talk about "peer pressure" as something negative. But it also has a positive side. When people feel affirmed and supported, they often respond by doing things that are positive and healthy.

It's important for everyone to feel accepted in your youth group. This "word relay race" gives group members a chance to express positive qualities they see in their peers.

How to Prepare

1. Read the "How to Lead" section to be sure you understand the activity.
2. Clear an open space in the middle of the room.

How to Lead

1. After the Bible study discussion, quickly form two teams with the same number of group members on each. If you have an extra person, ask one person to volunteer to be a judge.

2. Have both teams line up in the middle of the room, one person behind another.

3. Explain the game: We're going to play a word relay. The game's object is to say something positive about each of your fellow team members quicker than the other team can for each of its team members. Here's how it works:

● When I say "Go!" the person at the back of the line must say one reason it's easy to accept the person at the front of the line. For example, Terry might say, "It's easy to accept Melinda because she's always nice to everyone."

● As soon as the back person says something positive about the front person, the back person runs to the front of the line. The new back person must then give a positive reason about the new front person.

● You must follow three rules:

a. If someone on a team says something negative, the whole team must start over.

b. Team members can't give suggestions to other team members.

c. The front person must be able to hear the back person's affirmation.

● The first team finished wins.

4. Make sure everyone understands how to play. Then start the game. Keep the pace fast, and make sure everyone has fun and says something nice to another person.

5. Award the winning team the privilege of going through the refreshment line first.

Life Saver

What You'll Need

☐ Life-preservers made from construction paper
☐ Pencils
☐ Circle of chairs

Time Needed:

5 minutes

Sample 6-3
Sample Life-Preserver

From time to time, people all need support and encouragement. They may be going through a tough problem. Or they may need help with an important decision. As Christians, we can help people by being supportive and encouraging to them. We can also turn to God, who supports us when we ask for help.

This activity uses the symbol of a life-preserver to show how we can support each other.

 ## How to Prepare

1. Read the "How to Lead" section to be sure you understand the activity.
2. Gather the materials listed in the "What You'll Need" box.
3. Make round life-preservers out of pastel construction paper (see Sample 6-3). At the top of each preserver, draw a common Christian symbol such as a cross, fish or dove. Use your favorite symbol on all the life-preservers or use several different ones. Leave plenty of space for group members each to write their life goal on their life-preserver.
4. If you want, ask some friends to help you make the life-preservers.

 ## How to Lead

1. Gather group members together in a circle of chairs. Give each person a paper life-preserver and a pencil.
2. Then say: One reason it's important to be part of a group is that we can support each other, keeping each other afloat when life gets rough. So, in a way, we're all "life-preservers" for each other.

On the front of the paper life-preserver I gave you, write one way you can be a "life-preserver" for other people. You might write, for example, "I can be a life-preserver by calling people who miss a meeting."
3. Give group members a few minutes to write. Then say: While we can all be "life-preservers" for each other, we all need to be "rescued" sometimes, too. Turn over your paper life-preserver and write one time when you need other people to reach out to you. You might write, "I need someone to help me when life gets tough at home."
4. After group members have finished writing, ask them to volunteer to share what they wrote. Don't force anyone to share who is uncomfortable.
5. Then say: While we each support and comfort each other, our greatest support and comfort comes from God. As 2 Corinthians 1:3-4 says: "Praise be to the God and Father of our Lord Jesus Christ, . . . who comforts us in all our troubles, so that we can comfort those in any trouble with the comfort we ourselves have received from God."
6. Close with prayer, asking God to support and guide each person in the group so that everyone may, in turn, reach out and support others. Then join hands in a circle to sing one verse of "They Will Know We Are Christians by Our Love" (in *Songs* from Songs and Creations, Inc.).
7. Serve refreshments to the whole group. Let the affirmation winners go first.

Love or Money: Can We Have Both?

MEETING 7

Today's teenagers have lots of money. Each year they spend as much as $65 billion, and almost four out of 10 say they spend more than $30 per week. As a result, 93 percent of teenage girls say shopping is their favorite pastime.

With such an emphasis on money in teenagers' lives, it's important for Christian young people to keep a healthy perspective on money. This meeting encourages young people to think about their priorities and how to develop a balance in life.

Objectives

In this meeting, group members will:
● discover how much emphasis youth culture places on money;
● think about the priority love has over money;
● study what the Bible says about money and priorities; and
● affirm values in each other that are better than money can buy.

Biblical Foundation

Jesus frequently warned that money can rule a person instead of just being a means of fulfilling needs (Matthew 6:24). We're called on to use our resources and abilities to help those in need (Matthew 20:1-16; Matthew 25:34-40; and 1 John 3:17-18).

Adult Leader's Responsibilities

1. Meet with the meeting coordinator two weeks ahead of time. Help him or her find group members to lead each aspect of the meeting.

2. Call leaders several days in advance to ask if they have any questions and to be sure they have gathered all supplies and have prepared adequately.

Meeting Coordinator's Responsibilities

1. Photocopy the instructions for each part of the meeting to give to the leaders.

2. At least two weeks before the meeting, find a group member to lead each aspect of the meeting. (If you wish, you may lead one of the sections yourself.) Encourage leaders to find helpers if they need them.

3. Schedule a planning session with all leaders one week before the event to go through the meeting to be sure they understand it.

4. Find someone to coordinate refreshments for the meeting.

5. The day before the meeting, call all the leaders to make sure they're ready.

Meeting Outline				
Coordinator: _____				
Activity	Estimated Time	Who's Responsible	Telephone	Confirmed
Community-Builder: Shopping Spree	25 minutes			
Discussion-Starter: The Best That Money Can't Buy	10 minutes			
Learning Time: Love and Money	15 minutes			
Bible Study: Choosing Your Fortune	15 minutes			
Closing: I'd Like to Trade	5 minutes			
Refreshments				

Shopping Spree

What You'll Need

- ☐ Masking tape
- ☐ String
- ☐ Construction paper
- ☐ Scissors
- ☐ Glue
- ☐ Play money ($1,000 per person, plus some extra)
- ☐ Crayons
- ☐ Bucket or basket
- ☐ One copy of Handout 7-2
- ☐ Paper
- ☐ Pencils
- ☐ Letter-size envelopes (18)
- ☐ 3×5 cards
- ☐ A yard stick
- ☐ 20 chairs

Time Needed:

25 minutes

Don't you love to shop? Most teenagers do. This community-builder gives you a chance to go shopping and spend all the money you want without worrying about the cost. But can you really spend money without considering the consequences? We'll find out while playing "Shopping Spree."

How to Prepare

1. Find a friend or two to help you prepare for and set up the meeting.

2. Gather all the supplies listed in the "What You'll Need" box. You'll need three sheets of each color of construction paper: red, blue, green, pink, yellow and orange, plus two sheets of white paper. You'll also need enough red, blue, pink, green, yellow and orange crayons so everyone can have one crayon. Get the play money from board games such as Monopoly.

3. Read the "How to Lead" section to be sure you understand the activity. Also read the "Shopping Spree Rules" (Sample 7-4) and the "Shopping Options" cards (Handout 7-2).

4. Make construction paper signs for each store, using the colors and names designated in Sample 7-1. Tape a letter-size envelope on the bottom of each sign into which group members can deposit the money they spend in that store.

5. Cut out the descriptions in Handout 7-2, "Shopping Options," and paste them each on 3×5 cards.

6. Put the crayons in a bucket or basket.

7. Create a "mall" using the following steps and Sample 7-3, "Mall Layout" as guides. Give yourself plenty of time before the meeting:

● Create a rectangle-shape (12'×24') outline on the floor using masking tape.

● Mark 20, 3'×3' squares in the masking-tape rectangle. Use a yard stick to make it easy. Put four squares on each end and eight on each side (see Sample 7-3). Each of the 20 squares will be a store or the charity or the mall entrance or exit.

● Place chairs around the outside of the "mall" with one chair outside each "store." Label the mall entrance, exit, charity and the stores by taping the signs you made to the back of the chairs. Follow the order listed in Sample 7-3. Put the "Shopping Options" cards on the appropriate chairs.

Sample 7-1

Mall Shops

Write on separate sheets of *white* paper:
MALL ENTRANCE (Start Here)
CHARITY

Write on separate sheets of *blue* paper:
STEREO SOUND CENTER
NO-NAME JEAN COMPANY
MOVIE THEATER

Write on separate sheets of *green* paper:
CAR ACCESSORIES UNLIMITED
FASHION CENTER
EXIT (TIME TO GO HOME)

Write on separate sheets of *yellow* paper:
DESIGNER JEANS
FASHION WAREHOUSE
JUNK FOOD HAVEN

Write on separate sheets of *pink* paper:
BODY SHOP: SPORTS AND EXERCISE EQUIPMENT
FACTORY OUTLET
HAIR CUTTERS

Write on separate sheets of *orange* paper:
TOP-TEN RECORDS AND CDS
BOOKS, POSTERS AND MAGAZINES
JEWELRY AT ITS BEST

Write on separate sheets of *red* paper:
SHOES, SHOES, SHOES
BARGAIN EMPORIUM
IGLOO ICE CREAM

How to Lead

1. Begin the meeting by having group members line up at the mall entrance. Give each person paper and a pencil to use as a shopping list. Distribute to each group member $1,000 of play money in various denominations.

2. Explain the "Shopping Spree Rules" (Sample 7-4). Make sure group members understand, then start the game. After group members each have finished "shopping" at their first store, have them close their eyes. Let each group member pick a new crayon from the bucket or basket which you pass around. Continue until someone is ready to "go home."

3. When the game ends, have group members each total up the money they spent. Then ask:

● Did you spend your money for things you really needed or just for whatever was in the shop?

● Did you buy items because of their label or quality? Why?

● Was it okay to buy a no-label item if its quality was as good as the brand-name item? Explain.

● How much did you give to charity?

● Did you give any extra to charity, or just what the game required?

4. While you're discussing those questions, ask someone to gather the money from each envelope on the back of the signs. Have that person add up the money in each envelope, and report to the group members how much they spent together at each store. Ask:

● What do these totals tell us about our group's priorities and interests?

● Where do you think the group spent too much money? Why?

● Where should the group have spent more money? Why?

Sample 7-4

Shopping Spree Rules

1. Start at the mall entrance. Have your $1,000 and your shopping list (blank paper) ready. With your eyes closed, pick a crayon from the bucket or basket.

2. Go around the mall to your right until you reach the first store with the same color sign as your crayon.

3. Read the card in the store and decide what to do. If you decide to buy something, put the money in the envelope attached to the sign. Write on your shopping list what you bought and how much you spent.

4. When group members are ready, have them close their eyes and take another crayon from the basket, which you pass around. Continue around the mall using the crayon colors and the cards as your guide. Have people all move at the same time.

5. If you run out of money, return to the mall entrance. Collect only $500 this time, and start again. Try to be a wiser shopper next time!

6. The first person to land on the mall exit ends the game. If you're near the end of the mall and you draw a color that's not ahead of you, go backward to a shop with that color.

Shopping Options

Directions: Cut out each rectangle and glue it to a 3×5 card. Attach the card with string to the sign for that shop.

Charity
You're always welcome to donate as much as you like to charity.

Stereo Sound Center
1. The latest stereo system will cost you $600.
2. Buy a cheaper set for $150. (If you choose the cheaper set, go to the Factory Outlet to buy the stereo.)

No-Name Jean Company
1. Buy two pairs of no-name label jeans for $50.
2. Buy just one pair for $25, and pocket the savings.

Movie Theater
1. Take a friend to a movie for $20 (including popcorn, pop and candy).
2. Save your money and spend the time walking around the mall together.

Car Accessories Unlimited
1. A kit to spruce up your car is on sale for $25.
2. You think your car looks okay, so go to the charity space and donate the $25 to buy a winter coat for a needy child.

Fashion Center
The complete outfit you want to buy costs $600—which is actually a good price for an outfit from the latest hot fashion designer. If you still have $600, buy the outfit. If you don't have the money, return to the mall entrance, collect another $500 and start over.

Designer Jeans
1. All designer jeans sell for $80. Buy as many pairs as you wish.
2. Move to the No-Name Jean Company and buy one pair there.

Fashion Warehouse
Today's your lucky day. The store has a half-price sale. A gorgeous new winter coat is on sale for only $80. (It's regularly $160.) So you buy the coat. You may donate your savings ($80) to charity. But you don't have to. You decide.

Junk Food Haven
1. Buy a hamburger, drink and fries for $3.
2. Buy a small pizza and drink for $5.
3. Buy a deli turkey-and-cheese sandwich and cider for $2.
Whatever you buy, return to the "Charity" space and give what you think it would cost to feed one hungry person for an entire day.

Body Shop: Sports and Exercise Equipment
1. Buy exercise equipment to use at home for $500.
2. Give $50 to charity and move to Igloo Ice Cream to buy a treat instead.

Factory Outlet
The Factory Outlet has almost anything you want at half the price of other stores. But it also has long lines at the checkout counter.
1. You don't have to buy anything.
2. Sit out one turn and get bargain prices. You may buy a stereo ($150), jewelry ($25) or two cassette tapes ($10). Buy as many as you like.

Hair Cutters
1. Get the latest haircut and style for $100.
2. Get a regular haircut for $10.

Top-Ten Records and CDs
1. Buy your five favorite albums for $50.
2. Don't buy anything, but go to Books, Posters and Magazines to buy a book and a poster instead.

Books, Posters and Magazines
1. Buy a poster and a book for $15.
2. Don't buy anything, but stop at the library on the way home to check out two books.

Jewelry at Its Best
1. Buy a birthday present for your mom for $80.
2. Buy the same present at the Factory Outlet for only $25. If you choose this option, move back to the Factory Outlet and sit out a turn.

Shoes, Shoes, Shoes
1. You found the perfect shoes for prom night. But they cost $100. You can buy them if you want to.
2. Keep your old shoes and go to the Bargain Emporium and buy a $35 pair of shoes for a needy teenager.

Bargain Emporium
1. Buy two pairs of shoes for $35 each, and donate one pair to charity.
2. Just buy one inexpensive pair for yourself for $20.
3. Buy a $35 pair to donate to charity, and keep your old shoes.

Igloo Ice Cream
1. Treat yourself and a friend to an ice cream treat with giant cookies for $5.
2. Just look at all the goodies, but don't buy anything. Save the calories.

Mall Layout

12 feet

3 feet

3 feet

24 feet

Mall Entrance (Start Here)	Exit (Time to Go Home)	Junk Food Haven	Fashion Center

chair —

Stereo Sound Center			Jewelry at Its Best
Car Accessories Unlimited			Hair Cutters
Designer Jeans			Movie Theater
Body Shop: Sports and Exercise Equipment			Charity
Top-Ten Records and CDs			Factory Outlet
Shoes, Shoes, Shoes			Bargain Emporium
Fashion Warehouse	No-Name Jean Company	Igloo Ice Cream	Books, Posters and Magazines

The Best That Money Can't Buy

What You'll Need

☐ Copies of Handout 7-5
☐ Pencils
☐ Chairs

Time Needed:

10 minutes

If someone gave you a blank check and told you to fill it in for whatever amount of money it would take to make you happy, what amount would you write? This discussion-starter activity focuses on that question.

How to Prepare

1. Gather the supplies listed in the "What You'll Need" box.
2. Read the "How to Lead" section to be sure you understand the activity.
3. Make a copy of "Your Own Blank Check" (Handout 7-5) for each group member. Make a few extras just in case.

How to Lead

1. After the community-builder, tell the group members that today is their lucky day. You're going to give them each a blank check to fill in the amount of money it would take to make them happy.
2. Give group members each a check (Handout 7-5) and a pencil, and have them each fill out their check.
3. When everyone is finished, put the chairs in a circle for discussion. Ask volunteers each to share what they wrote on their check.

Handout 7-5

Your Own Blank Check

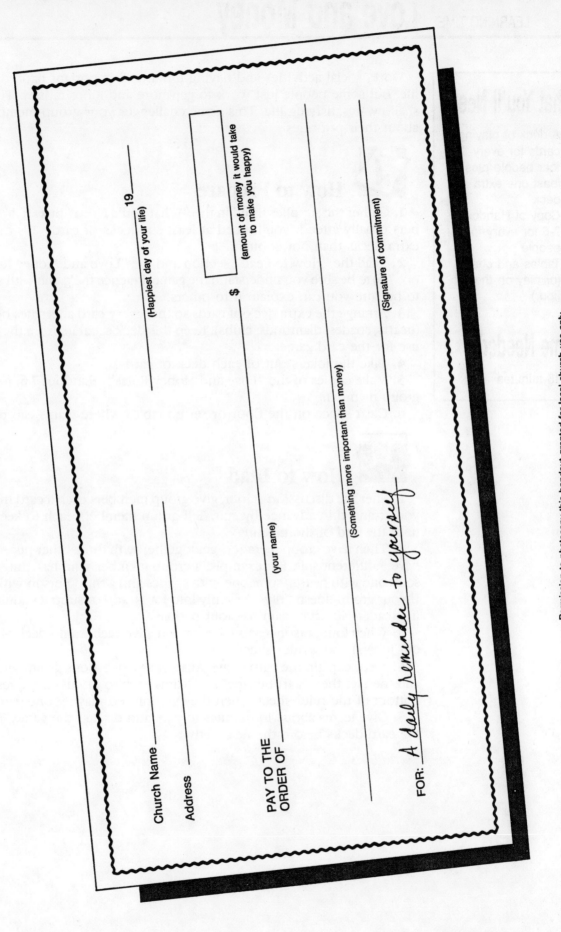

Church Name _____

Address _____

19 ___

(Happiest day of your life)

PAY TO THE
ORDER OF _____

(your name)

$ [   ]

(amount of money it would take
to make you happy)

_____

(Something more important than money)

_____

(Signature of commitment)

FOR: *A daily reminder to yourself*

Love and Money

What You'll Need

- ☐ A deck of playing cards for every four people plus at least one extra deck
- ☐ Copy of Handout 7-6 for every four people
- ☐ Tables and chairs (or play on the floor)

Time Needed:

15 minutes

Work, social activities and having fun are all important parts of a balanced life. But some people just work to get more and more money. The result is a shallow, unsatisfying life. This game challenges your group members to think about their priorities.

 ## How to Prepare

1. Gather the supplies listed in the "What You'll Need" box. If 24 group members usually attend, you'll need at least six decks of cards. It's better to have extra decks than not enough.

2. Read the "How to Lead" section and the "Love and Money Rules" (Handout 7-6) to be sure you understand the game. Practice the game with some friends to be sure you can explain it to others.

3. Arrange the extra deck of cards so that every card alternates between suits (hearts, spades, diamonds, clubs). Keep this deck separate from the decks you'll use for the card game.

4. Take the jokers out of each deck of cards.

5. Make copies of the "Love and Money Rules" (Handout 7-6) for every four group members.

6. Clear space on the floor or set up tables where teams can play cards.

 ## How to Lead

1. After the discussion-starter, give group members each a card from the deck you arranged in advance by suit. Tell group members each to keep their card until the end of the meeting.

2. Then have group members get together with three other people who each have a different suit. For example, a group member who has clubs would find someone with hearts, someone with spades and a third person with diamonds. If your group doesn't divide evenly into fours, add or subtract adults and meeting leaders so each team has four people.

3. When four-person teams have formed, give each team a deck of cards (without jokers) and a rules sheet.

4. Next, explain the card game. Answer any questions group members have, and then let them start playing. Ask teams each to discuss the questions at the bottom of the rules sheet when they've finished playing one game.

5. Give teams about 10 minutes to play and discuss the game. Then collect the card decks before the next activity.

Love and Money Rules

The game's object is to collect as many hearts and spades as possible, while getting rid of as many diamonds as possible. You earn and lose points based on the cards you collect:
- Hearts represent *love*. They earn the most points.
- Spades represent *work*. They only earn half as many points as hearts.
- Clubs represent the *social activities*. They neither help nor hurt your score because they have no point value.
- Diamonds stand for *money*. You lose points for every diamond you collect.

Here are the cards' point values:

	Hearts	Spades	Diamonds
Ace	+30	+15	-50
King	+20	+10	-30
Queen	+20	+10	-30
Jack	+10	+5	-20
Ten and lower	+face value	+half face value	-face value

1. Deal each player 10 cards. Stack the remaining cards face down on the table. Turn the top card face up.

2. The group member on the dealer's left begins. Each player must lay down a card with either the same number or suit as the face-up card on the table. Go around the table for one round.

3. If you can't lay down a card, draw a card from the deck. If you can play that card, do so. If not, keep it in your hand and pass to the next person.

4. The person who lays down the highest card collects all five cards. If the card from the deck was highest, no one gets the hand. Put the cards from that round on the bottom of the deck.

5. The game ends when a group member gets rid of all the diamonds in his or her hand. Then count up each player's points using the table on this sheet. The group member with the highest score wins.

After the game, discuss these questions as a team:
1. Do you agree with the values this game places on each area of life (love, work, social activities and money)? Why or why not?

2. How important should love and money be in our lives?

3. Does love always help us and money always hurt us? Why or why not?

4. What are ways we can keep each of these areas in proper balance?

Choosing Your Fortune

What You'll Need

- ☐ Newsprint
- ☐ Markers
- ☐ Tape
- ☐ Bibles
- ☐ Paper
- ☐ Pencils
- ☐ Chairs

Time Needed:

15 minutes

Have you ever played a game where teams tried to guess a missing word or phrase, each team guessing one letter at a time until one team could guess the entire phrase? This is how "Choosing Your Fortune" works, except you are guessing a phrase from the Bible.

This activity tells what the Bible says about money and love and how important they should rate in our lives and daily duties.

How to Prepare

1. Gather the supplies listed in the "What You'll Need" box.

2. Read the "How to Lead" section to be sure you understand the activity.

3. Tape together two or three sheets of newsprint. Precisely copy the following lines only (not the number of spaces written underneath) onto the sheets of newsprint. Leave space between words as indicated:

"___ _____ _____ ____ ___
(3 spaces) (6 spaces) (5 spaces) (4 spaces) (3 spaces)

___ _____."
(3 spaces) 5 spaces)

4. Double-check to make sure the lines and spaces you drew fit the phrase "You cannot serve both God and Money," which is from Matthew 6:24 (New International Version).

5. On a separate sheet of newsprint, write the following Bible references as clues: Matthew 20:1-16; Matthew 25:34-40; and 1 John 3:17-18.

6. Make a copy of Sample 7-7 "Clue Sheet" to help you quickly find where various letters fit in the puzzle and how many times each letter appears.

7. Write the following questions on newsprint. Be sure not to let anyone see them before the final discussion in the Bible study.

● Is it true that you can't love both God and money? Why or why not?

● What are ways we try to serve both God and money?

● Do teenagers today worry too much about what they eat and wear? Why or why not?

● What do you think this passage tells us about how we earn and spend money?

● How does sharing money with people in need fit with the passage?

How to Lead

1. After the card game, tape the sheets of newsprint with the missing phrase on the wall. Also tape a blank sheet of newsprint nearby where you can list all the incorrect letters group members guess. Also tape on the wall the newsprint with the Bible verse clues.

2. Tell group members each to look at the card they received before the card game and get together with everyone else who has a card of the same suit (all hearts together, all diamonds together and so forth). Have teams each sit together in chairs or on the floor where they can see the newsprint.

3. Make sure everyone has a Bible.

4. Say: The blanks on the newsprint represent the words in a phrase from the Bible. The Bible references on the other sheet are clues to the phrase, but the phrase doesn't come from them.

Each team will take turns guessing the letters in the puzzle. If your team guesses a letter correctly, I'll write the letter in the puzzle however many times it appears. If your team chooses a letter that's in the puzzle, you get another turn. But if the letter isn't in the puzzle, I'll write it on the blank sheet of newsprint, and the next team gets a chance.

If your team thinks you know the whole phrase, you may guess it when it's your turn. The guess must be exactly right to win.

5. Begin the game by letting the "hearts" go first. If the team chooses a correct letter, write it with a marker on the newsprint in the appropriate place or places. Refer to your clue sheet whenever you need to.

6. When the team guesses a wrong letter, add it to the incorrect letter sheet.

7. When a team thinks it knows the entire phrase, it may guess. The guess must be completely correct to get credit. Don't write in any letters when a guess is wrong—even if the team missed only one word.

8. After the puzzle is finished, have each team read the verse in its context in Matthew 6:24-34. Post the newsprint with the discussion questions and answer the questions. Give each team paper and pencils to take notes.

9. After the teams have discussed the questions, bring the whole group together in a circle and have teams report on what they learned.

Sample 7-7

Clue Sheet

YOU CANNOT SERVE BOTH GOD AND MONEY

A=2	B=1	C=1	D=2	E=3	G=1
H=1	M=1	N=4	O=5	R=1	S=1
T=2	U=1	V=1	Y=2		

What You'll Need

☐ Chairs

Time Needed:

5 minutes

Some things money can't buy. And most often, these things are the most valuable possessions in life. We all have some of these valuable things within us. They're gifts from God.

In this activity, group members will affirm things about each other that are better than money can buy—patience, friendliness, compassion—by "trading" these valuable possessions with each other.

 ## How to Prepare

1. Gather the supplies listed in the "What You'll Need" box.

2. Read the "How to Lead" section to be sure you understand the activity.

3. Practice your introduction to the activity. You don't have to use the exact words; say what you think will be meaningful for your group.

4. Choose a song, such as "Day by Day" from *Godspell*.

 ## How to Lead

1. After the Bible study, divide the group in half. Have the hearts and diamonds form one group and the clubs and spades form another. Both groups need to be exactly the same size. If you have an extra group member, ask an adult sponsor to join one team.

2. Have one team form a circle of chairs and sit down, facing inward. Then have the other team members each stand behind one of the seated group members. (Be sure you're in the standing circle.)

3. Then explain the activity: Sometimes we think we can buy everything we need or want. But many of the most important things in life don't have price tags. They're qualities that money can't buy.

In the past, people have gotten things they needed by trading. For example, a farmer might trade a fast racing horse for a strong horse that could pull a wagon. Or a woman might do someone's laundry for a new dress she couldn't afford.

In this activity, we're symbolically going to trade qualities with each other—qualities that money can't buy. You're going to trade a positive trait with your partner who's sitting in front of you or standing behind you. You'll ask to trade for something internal you wish you had more of (such as patience, kindness or humility). To show how it works, I'll go first.

4. Begin the affirmations by talking about your partner. Put your hands on your partner's shoulders and say something positive you'd like to trade with him or her. You could say, for example, "I'd like to trade some of my enthusiasm for Carey's patience because she always takes the time to do things right."

5. Then give standing group members each a chance to "trade."

6. When all the standing group members have spoken, have partners trade places. The new standing group members each do the same thing, saying something like: "I'd be glad to trade Jan some of my patience, if she'd trade me her pretty smile. She always makes everyone feel welcome."

7. Give each group member a chance to share. Then close by holding hands in a circle and singing a verse of "Day by Day" from *Godspell* (in *Songs*, from Songs and Creations, Inc.) or another favorite song.

8. Close with your group's traditional closing or pray together, asking God to help you keep priorities straight and view money through his eyes. Send group members home with their checks as reminders of what's really important in life.

9. Break for refreshments.

What Do You Believe?

It's easy to call ourselves Christians, go to church, attend youth group meetings and even participate in mission trips without really knowing what we believe. Yet it's important for Christians to know what they believe and be able to articulate those beliefs.

This meeting is designed to help group members think about and write statements of their Christian beliefs. In the process of writing and discussing their ideas, they learn more about their faith.

Objectives

In this meeting, group members will:
- interview each other about what they believe;
- write letters summarizing their faith;
- do a crossword puzzle that helps them discover central themes in Christianity;
- choose statements of faith that represent their beliefs;
- write headlines that summarize different expressions of faith; and
- summarize their beliefs in a single phrase.

Biblical Foundation

The Bible study crossword puzzle refers group members to numerous Bible passages that focus on Christian principles.

Adult Leader's Responsibilities

1. Meet with the meeting coordinator two weeks ahead of time. Help the coordinator find group members to lead each aspect of the meeting.

2. Call meeting leaders several days in advance to ask if they have any questions and to be sure they have gathered all supplies and have prepared adequately.

3. If the group is interested in actually publishing the letters, work with the meeting coordinator to arrange production, printing and mailing.

Meeting Coordinator's Responsibilities

1. Make a photocopy of the instructions for each part of the meeting to give to the leaders.

2. At least two weeks before the meeting, find group members to lead different aspects of the meeting. (If you wish, you may lead one of the sections yourself.) Give leaders each a photocopy of the meeting element they're leading. Encourage leaders to find helpers if needed.

3. Schedule a planning session one week before the event with all leaders to go through the meeting and be sure every leader understands it. Since the various meeting elements revolve around the letters group members write during the learning time, it's important that all leaders work together on this meeting.

4. Find someone to coordinate refreshments to serve between the learning time and the Bible study.

5. The day before the meeting, call all the leaders to make sure they're ready for the meeting. Go over the activity with each leader to make sure he or she hasn't forgotten any details.

6. Consider actually editing and printing the make-believe newsletter that provides the meeting's focus. After the meeting, recruit group members to help with editing, typing and layout. Ask the church office to help with printing. Then find volunteers to help prepare a mailing. Send the newsletter to group members and parents—and anyone else who might be interested.

Meeting Outline

Coordinator: _____

Activity	Estimated Time	Who's Responsible	Telephone	Confirmed
Community-Builder: On the Beat	10 minutes			
Learning Time: Letters to the Editor	15 minutes			
Refreshments				
Bible Study: Editors Meeting	25 minutes			
Affirmation: Good News Headlines	5 minutes			
Closing: I Believe	5 minutes			

On the Beat

What You'll Need

- ☐ Copies of "Interview Questions," (Handout 8-1)
- ☐ Pencils
- ☐ Chairs or floor pillows
- ☐ Paper or toy telephones

Time Needed:

10 minutes

What does it mean to be a Christian? Why do you go to church? This activity is your opportunity to think about such questions.

How to Prepare

1. Gather the supplies listed in the "What You'll Need" box. Set up the chairs or pillows in pairs so group members can sit back to back.

2. Read the "How to Lead" section to be sure you understand the activity.

3. Make a copy of Handout 8-1, "Interview Questions," for each pair of group members. Cut the handout in half so each group member in the pair has different questions.

4. Make paper telephone receivers for group members, use toy telephones or just pretend to talk on the phone.

How to Lead

1. When it's time to start the meeting, have group members each find a partner—someone they don't know well. If you have an extra person, form one trio. Have partners sit back to back in chairs or on the floor.

2. Give each pair Handout 8-1, with each group member getting one set of questions. Also distribute pencils.

3. Ask one group member in each pair to start by pretending to call his or her partner on the telephone, following the format listed on the handout. Have the interviewer ask questions, and jot notes on the interview. Allow about two minutes.

4. Then have group members switch roles so the other person can conduct an interview using the other set of questions. Allow another two minutes.

5. Bring the group back together, and have pairs each tell something interesting about their interview.

Interview Questions

Interviewer 1	Interviewer 2
1. Do you enjoy going to church? Why or why not?	**1.** How would you describe your church to someone who doesn't know anything about Christianity?
2. What's your favorite part of the worship service?	**2.** What single characteristic distinguishes Christians from adherents to other faiths?
3. If you could change anything about your church, what would you change? Why?	**3.** Do you think it's helpful to learn about other religions? Why or why not?
4. If you were inviting someone to come to church with you, how would you describe your church?	**4.** If someone from another country, culture and religion visited your school, what would you tell that person about your church?
5. How do you think your church views your youth group?	**5.** How would you describe your worship service to someone from another country?

LEARNING TIME: Letters to the Editor

What You'll Need

☐ Bibles
☐ Paper
☐ Pencils
☐ Bible dictionary
☐ Concordance
☐ Tables and chairs

Time Needed:

15 minutes

Sometimes we can "think better on paper." By writing things down, a better understanding of what we think and believe. In this activity, group members will think about what they believe as Christians and will write a statement of their faith.

How to Prepare

1. Gather the supplies listed in the "What You'll Need" box.
2. Read the "How to Lead" section to be sure you understand the activity. Practice making a dramatic entrance to explain the activity. You don't have to use the exact words that are suggested; say what's natural for you.
3. Set up tables where group members can work.
4. Meet with the Bible study leader to coordinate the learning time with the Bible study.
5. Wait outside the meeting room during the community-builder.

How to Lead

1. After the community-builder, get group members' attention by running into the room, acting like you're out of breath and shouting: Stop the presses! Stop the presses!
2. Stand in the middle of the group, panting and trying to catch your breath. Then explain what has happened. You could say:

I'm sorry to interrupt your meeting, but I have an urgent request. I'm a columnist for Christians International Newsletter, and I just found out today that I have to write a special piece telling teenagers around the world what it means to be a Christian. The problem is I only have half an hour. I know you're busy, but could you please help?

Here's what I need: I want to show how diverse Christianity is, so I need to present a lot of different perspectives. I would run a national contest to find out what people believe, but I don't have time. So I need each of you to write something. We can have a mini-contest right here.

3. Distribute paper and pencils to group members. Ask them to enter the newsletter contest by writing a short statement of what they believe. It can be as short as a sentence or as long as a page. They can use the Bible reference books you have, and they can include scripture passages. But they only have 10 minutes—it's a tight deadline. Tell group members not to sign their letters—they should be completely anonymous.
4. When group members have all turned in their papers, close the activity by telling the group that the winning entries will be posted after the editors decide which letters to print.
5. After this activity, serve refreshments to give everyone a break.
6. Give the letters to the person leading the Bible study.

Editors Meeting

What You'll Need

- ☐ Bibles
- ☐ Letters from the learning time
- ☐ Pencils
- ☐ Tables and chairs
- ☐ Copy of "Bible Study Crossword Puzzle," (Handout 8-2), for every five people

Time Needed:

25 minutes

Sample 8-3
"Bible Crossword Puzzle" Key

While it's important for each of us to know what we personally believe, it's also important to talk about our faith with other Christians. In the previous activity ("Letters to the Editor"), group members each wrote a letter explaining what they believe as Christians. This activity uses those letters to help group members discuss their beliefs together. The crossword puzzle introduces some basic Christian beliefs. These will help group members evaluate the letters.

 ## How to Prepare

1. Gather the supplies listed in the "What You'll Need" box. Supply several different Bible translations to help with the crossword puzzle.

2. Read the "How to Lead" section to be sure you understand the activity.

3. Think of "editorial departments" to divide your group into. You'll need one department for every five group members who attend. Some departments might include city news, national news, international news, sports, business or fashion.

4. Practice what you'll say during the Bible study and "editors meeting." You don't have to use the exact words that are suggested; say what's natural for you.

5. Meet with the learning time leader to coordinate the learning time with the Bible study.

6. Have the key for the crossword puzzle (Sample 8-3) handy during the meeting, but don't show it to anyone.

 ## How to Lead

1. After the refreshment time, say: I have good news. I just learned from the publisher that all group members here have been promoted from writers to editors. Congratulations! I have new assignments for each person, so listen up.

Then divide the group into "editorial departments," with five group members in each department. Give each department a table where it can work, and distribute Bibles to group members who don't have them.

2. When group members are settled, announce that it's time for an editorial meeting. And since this is a religious newsletter, you want to begin the meeting with a short Bible study. Mention that today's Bible study is also a chance to test a crossword puzzle you want to include in the next newsletter.

3. Distribute pencils and a copy of Handout 8-2, "Bible Study Crossword Puzzle," to each department. Allow about 10 minutes to work the puzzle. If group members have trouble with particular words, have them look in different Bible translations. Often a different translation will have the key word to solve the puzzle.

4. When all the departments have finished the puzzle, answer any questions group members have. Then say it's time to get back to work and make some editorial decisions.

5. Randomly distribute five letters from the learning time to each department. Explain that you need to decide which letters to publish. Unfortunately, you don't have much space, so you can only print one letter from each department. Each department must read its five letters, then evaluate and select just one letter from the five.

6. Before evaluations start, suggest that each department set "editorial standards" to help with the letter evaluation. These standards might include:

- Must be well-written.
- Must be easy to read.

- Must have meaning for someone who reads it.

Suggest these or other possibilities, but let each department set its own standards. Also suggest that group members use in their evaluations the scriptural principles from the puzzle.

In their evaluation process, urge groups not to be very critical of the letters. They should focus on the faith affirmations in the letters and emphasize the positive characteristics in the best letters.

7. Allow about 10 minutes for discussion.

8. After each department has chosen one letter, bring the whole "staff" together. Have each department read its choice, tell why it chose the letter, and why the editors feel it would be good for the newsletter.

9. If you have time, ask the editors about the evaluation process:
- Was it difficult to choose the letters? Why or why not?
- How did the crossword puzzle help with the decision?
- How did establishing "editorial standards" help?
- If they were rewriting their letters now, what would they do differently?

10. Thank the departments for their hard work. Mark the letters that were chosen. Then collect all the letters to pass on to the affirmation leader.

Bible Study Crossword Puzzle

Across

2. _____ are responsible for your own actions. (James 2:14-18)
3. God offers forgiveness for any _____. (1 John 2:1-6)
9. The three greatest principles of the Christian faith are faith, hope and _____. (1 Corinthians 13:1-13)
10. God will _____ us if we forgive others. (Matthew 6:14-15)
12. We should give _____ to God in everything we do. (Colossians 3:17)
14. It is our responsibility to _____ with those in need—not only food and clothes, but also love and kindness. (Matthew 25:35-40)
16. _____ gives us confidence in our faith. (2 Corinthians 3:4-6)
17. John the Baptist was described as a _____ man. (Luke 1:15)
18. _____ is full of temptations. (John 14:6 and 1 John 2:16-17)
19. You must _____ the truth with kind words. (Ephesians 4:25-32)
21. Jesus said the two greatest _____ were to love God and love your neighbor as yourself. (Matthew 22:37-40)
22. Strive to do good in your life; do not give in to drinking _____ and other strong drinks. (Titus 2:1-3)

Down

1. God asks that we do _____, love mercy and walk humbly with our God. (Micah 6:8)
4. Jesus said the poor in spirit, the meek, the peacemakers, the persecuted and the pure in heart are _____. (Matthew 5:3-10)
5. You must always work for _____. (Romans 14:19)
6. _____ said it is important to know the truth. (John 8:31-32)
7. Jesus told the disciples to _____ and teach the gospel. (Mark 16:15)
8. Sometimes we all feel too _____ to resist peer pressure but through our faith we can find strength. (Romans 15:1-2)
10. _____ cannot be bought or won with favors. (John 15:12-13)
11. Because God loved us and sent his Son, we can have _____ life. (John 3:16)
13. Jesus said that the people should repent with kindness toward others instead of animal _____. (Matthew 9:9-13)
15. _____ to God in private. (Matthew 6:5-8)
16. When you _____ to others, make sure it's not for glory or praise. (Matthew 6:2-4)
19. Jesus Christ is the _____ of God. (Hebrews 1:1-7)
20. We are not _____ by what we do, but by grace. (Ephesians 2:1-10)

AFFIRMATION: Good News Headlines

The first thing people read in a newspaper story is the headline. The headline tells what the story's about, and it grabs the reader's attention. In this activity group members will write headlines for your newsletter. Their headlines will share the "Good News."

What You'll Need

☐ Letters from the learning time
☐ Pencils

Time Needed:

5 minutes

How to Prepare

1. Gather the supplies listed in the "What You'll Need" box.
2. Read the "How to Lead" section to be sure you understand the activity.
3. Coordinate with the other meeting leaders to let them know you'll need the letters from their activities.
4. Practice what you'll say to announce the activity. You don't have to use the exact words that are suggested; say what's natural for you.

How to Lead

1. Start the activity with a lively introduction. Have a friend leave the room during the Bible study. Then when it's time to start the affirmation, have him or her come to the door and call you over to whisper something in your ear. When you hear it, get excited. Then go back to the group and say: Good news group members! The publisher has just changed her mind. She read all the letters and decided to publish every one of them—not just the ones the editorial departments selected. We've decided to devote the whole newsletter to the letters!
2. Then randomly distribute a letter and pencil to each group member.
3. Next, say: Since we're including all the letters, we need to write a headline for each one. We need each group member to think of three or four words that capture the essence of the letter. Headlines need to be positive eye-catchers that will encourage people to read the letter. I have a headline here that illustrates the kind of headline we're looking for: "Knowing Christ Brings Peace." We only have a few minutes before we go to press, so please work quickly.
4. Allow two or three minutes for writing. Then ask group members each to share their headline with the whole group. Collect the letters after they've been read.
5. After the activity, pass the letters on to the closing leader.

CLOSING: **I Believe**

The early Christians summarized their faith in the confession "Jesus is Lord." This activity draws together everything group members have said about their faith and captures their joint confession of faith in a single phrase that says what they believe as Christians.

What You'll Need

☐ A cover for your group's newsletter
☐ Letters from the learning time
☐ Newsprint
☐ A marker
☐ Stapler

Time Needed:

5 minutes

How to Prepare

1. Gather the supplies listed in the "What You'll Need" box.
2. Read the "How to Lead" section to be sure you understand the activity.
3. Coordinate with the other meeting leaders to let them know you'll need the letters from their activities.
4. Design a cover for the special edition of your group's newsletter. Leave space for the group to decide a title. See Sample 8-4 "Newsletter Cover." If your youth group publishes a regular newsletter, use its logo and design if you like.

How to Lead

1. Immediately after the affirmation, tell the group members that the only job left is to decide a title for this special edition of the newsletter. To do this, you're going to brainstorm titles as a group.
2. Post the newsprint where everyone can see it. Ask group members to suggest titles.
3. When you have five or six suggestions, have group members discuss the options to decide which is best. If they can't agree on one title, try combining elements from different titles to make one that everybody likes.
4. When you've settled on a title, write it on the cover you brought, and staple the cover with all the letters to form your "newsletter."
5. Sing a song together that celebrates your faith. "Amazing Grace," "The Doxology" or "Father, We Adore You" (in *Songs*, from Songs and Creations, Inc.) would be appropriate.
6. Conclude the meeting by leading a group prayer. Have group members pray sentence prayers, thanking God for the faith he has given us. After several group members have prayed, close the prayer, thanking God for the gifts he has given us and for sending his Son to be our Savior.

Sample 8-4
Newsletter Cover

Is Anybody Out There?

Youth suicide is a tragic problem in the United States. It is the third leading cause of death among teenagers. Almost half of all high school honor students say they know someone who has attempted or committed suicide, and 31 percent say they have considered it themselves.

Yet suicide is usually preventable. While professional help is critical for someone with suicidal tendencies, anyone can help prevent it by being a loving, kind and supportive friend. By reaching out to people around us before they become suicidal, we may help save lives.

This meeting introduces group members to the problem of suicide and helps them deal with their own frustrations and needs before their frustrations become serious.

Objectives

In this meeting, group members will:
- play a game that simulates how they deal with stress;
- write anonymous letters asking for advice;
- work together to help each other with problems;
- discover some of the warning signs of suicide;
- make sculptures to represent how they feel about themselves and what they think Jesus wants them to become; and
- help each other see positive characteristics within themselves.

Biblical Foundation

One of the central needs of suicidal people is to feel okay about who they are. The Bible study focuses on Jesus' teaching that it's okay—sometimes even desirable—to be different (Matthew 6:1-15; Matthew 23:13-27; and John 8:1-11, 15).

Adult Leader's Responsibilities

1. Meet with the meeting coordinator at least two weeks ahead of time. Help the coordinator find group members to lead different aspects of the meeting.

2. Call meeting leaders three or four days in advance to ask if they have any questions and to be sure they have gathered all supplies and have prepared adequately.

3. Help the learning time leader gather resources about suicide, including local contacts for people who fear a friend might be suicidal or who might feel suicidal themselves.

4. Because you're dealing with a serious topic, be prepared to address any critical issues that arise during the meeting.

Meeting Coordinator's Responsibilities

1. Make a photocopy of the instructions for each part of the meeting to give to the leaders.

2. At least two weeks before the meeting, find a group member to lead each aspect of the meeting. (If you wish, you may lead one of the sections yourself.) Give leaders each a photocopy of the meeting element they're leading. Encourage leaders to find helpers if needed.

3. Schedule a planning session one week before the event with all leaders to go through the meeting to be sure everyone understands it.

4. Find someone to coordinate refreshments to serve after the meeting.

5. The day before the meeting, call all the leaders to make sure they're ready for the meeting. Go over the activity with each leader to make sure he or she hasn't forgotten any details.

Meeting Outline

Coordinator: _____

Activity	Estimated Time	Who's Responsible	Telephone	Confirmed
Community-Builder: Panic Game	20 minutes			
Learning Time: I Need Help	15 minutes			
Bible Study: Sculptures	15 minutes			
Affirmation: Mirror Image	5 minutes			
Closing: Togetherness	5 minutes			
Refreshments				

COMMUNITY-BUILDER: Panic Game

What You'll Need

☐ Wooden building blocks
☐ A clear space on the floor

Time Needed:

20 minutes

Have you ever wished for a panic button you could push that would make your worries disappear? Unfortunately, no such devise is available. But we can learn to cope with our problems, reducing our sense of panic.

The "Panic Game" will help your group have fun and begin to share feelings about what causes them stress.

How to Prepare

1. Gather the supplies listed in the "What You'll Need" box. You can probably borrow the wooden blocks from children's Sunday school rooms. Try to get different shapes and sizes—long rectangles, squares, columns, little blocks, large blocks, and at least one or two triangles. You need at least one block per person.

2. Read the "How to Lead" section to be sure you understand the activity.

3. Clear a large space on an uncarpeted floor where the group can build block towers.

How to Lead

1. Invite group members to join you in a circle on the floor as they arrive for the meeting. Have the blocks sitting on the floor in the middle of the circle.

2. When group members have all arrived, say: Different people panic in different ways when they're under stress. Let's begin our meeting by each picking a block that symbolizes how we usually panic. For example, if you're the kind of person who panics over everything, you might pick the smallest block you can find because it doesn't take much to get you to panic. Or if you feel like a roller coaster—up and down, up and down—you might pick a triangle which goes up to a point and then just drops off to nothing. Look around and find the block that best describes how you handle panicky times.

3. Don't give people much time to choose their blocks. Keep saying: Hurry, hurry. We don't have much time. Then have group members each briefly tell why they selected a particular block. Push them to talk quickly so you don't "waste" any time. (You want to create a feeling of panic.)

4. Next, divide the group into three teams with roughly the same number of group members on each team. Have them stay on the floor.

5. Explain that you're going to play a game called "Panic." The object of the game is for all three teams to build a tall block tower together. One person from each team must place a block on the tower in turn. Each block must go right on *top* of (not beside) the block before it. Thus, someone from team one puts down a block followed by someone from team two followed by someone from team three. Then another person from team one places a block, and so on.

Group members must work as fast and as carefully as possible. If the tower falls, everyone must retrieve his or her block and start again. When everyone has placed a block, the game ends. If someone puts a block on top of the tower that no one can put a block on top of (such as a triangle), then the game ends because no one else can play.

6. When everyone understands the game, begin with the first team. Create a feeling of panic by pushing group members to go faster and faster. Allow no more than five minutes for the game. If the tower isn't finished by then, stop anyway.

7. Finally, form a circle for discussion. Ask:

● How did you feel when the tower fell?

● How did you feel when the triangle was placed on the tower?

● How did you feel being pressured to work so fast when you were trying to balance little blocks on a tower?

● If you had a big block, how did you feel if someone right before you put a little block on the tower?

● What did you learn about yourself through the activity?

I Need Help

How can we show we care? One way is to listen—really listen—to what people say. This letter-writing exercise is designed to help group members stop and listen to others and think about the problem of teenage suicide.

What You'll Need

☐ Paper
☐ Pencils
☐ Addresses and phone numbers for local suicide prevention organizations
☐ Brochures about suicide
☐ Chairs

Time Needed:

15 minutes

How to Prepare

1. Gather the supplies listed in the "What You'll Need" box. Check with local hospitals, counselors, educators or counseling hotlines to gather information on the warning signs of suicide. Ask for enough copies for everyone in your youth group.

2. Read the "How to Lead" section to be sure you understand the activity. Read the brochures you receive about suicide. Think of how you would summarize the main points. If you have questions, talk to your pastor or youth minister.

3. Work with your pastor or youth minister to develop a list of addresses and phone numbers of local people group members can contact if they're worried that a friend might be thinking about suicide. Type up the list and copy it for group members.

How to Lead

1. After the "Panic Game" discussion, have group members sit in a circle of chairs. Begin the learning time by reading aloud "Franklin's Story" (Sample 9-1).

2. Give each group member a piece of paper and a pencil. Then say: Have you ever felt totally frustrated and helpless? Have you ever felt like nothing ever works out the way you want it to? Or that no one listens to you? Today there is someone who will listen to you. You're going to write an anonymous letter to an advice column called "Dear Help."

On the paper I gave you, briefly tell what problem is bothering you that you'd like help with. Don't use real names; use only fictitious names if you feel like you need to use any names. You have about five minutes to write your letter.

3. When people finish, collect all the letters.

4. Have each group member find a partner to work with and a place where they can work together. Shuffle the letters. Then give each pair two letters.

5. Have each pair read its two letters and decide what advice to give. Remind group members that these are important issues, so they should take them seriously. Insist that no one ridicule a letter. Allow about five minutes.

6. When time is up, bring group members back into a circle. Have the pairs describe their letters and what advice they'd give.

7. Distribute copies of any brochures you received about suicide. Summarize and discuss the main points as a group. Be sure to talk about the best ways to be helpful. Emphasize that people should talk to a pastor, youth minister, school counselor or other professional trained in suicide prevention if they suspect that they or a friend might have warning signs of suicide.

Franklin's Story

Everyone sat in shocked silence. Monday morning the principal asked that we all pause for a moment of silence for Franklin, an 18-year-old senior who had committed suicide over the weekend. We all sat shocked. "Franklin? Why would Franklin want to kill himself? I didn't even know he was upset."

What can we do to help people like Franklin before they become depressed and begin contemplating suicide? We can help by showing that we genuinely care through our actions.

We can't solve another person's problems for them. Nor are we responsible for what someone else does. We are only responsible for our own actions. But we can all listen and be kind to others.

BIBLE STUDY: # Sculptures

What You'll Need

☐ Reusable play clay
☐ Tables
☐ Newsprint
☐ Marker
☐ Bibles
☐ Chairs

Time Needed:

15 minutes

People who try to commit suicide often feel like they aren't valuable—that no one likes them the way they are. They usually don't like themselves or something about themselves. This Bible study reminds group members that it's okay—sometimes even better—to be different from those around them. It also makes them realize that they can change things about their personalities that they don't like. This gives them hope for the future so they don't give up.

 ## How to Prepare

1. Gather the supplies listed in the "What You'll Need" box. You'll need two chunks of reusable clay for each group member. You can buy it, make your own (recipes are in many craft books) or borrow some from children's Sunday school classrooms.

2. Read the "How to Lead" section to be sure you understand the activity.

3. Write the following Bible references on newsprint to display during the activity:

- Matthew 6:1-15
- Matthew 23:13-27
- John 8:1-11, 15

 ## How to Lead

1. After the learning time, ask group members to sit around tables. Give each person a piece of clay.

2. Then ask group members each to create a clay sculpture that symbolizes their personality. Give an example: You might sculpt an electrical outlet with 10 wires plugged in it because you always feel so frantic and busy. Allow group members about five minutes to sculpt.

3. Post the newsprint with the three Bible references. Have group members read the verses to themselves.

4. Then give group members each their second piece of clay. Have them make another sculpture to depict the kind of person Jesus challenges us to become. For example, someone could make a hand because Jesus calls us to reach out to others. Allow another five minutes to sculpt.

5. When everyone is finished, form a circle and have volunteers explain their sculptures. Ask them to compare their two sculptures and share their similarities or differences. If group members don't volunteer without prompting, say things like: Who else would like to share a sculpture with us? or I'm really interested in your's, Jane. Can you tell us about it?

AFFIRMATION: # Mirror Image

What You'll Need

☐ A hand-held mirror
☐ Circle of chairs

Time Needed:

5 minutes

One way to feel better about ourselves is to hear others say—and really mean—kind words about us. Unfortunately, though, we're more likely to hear what we do wrong or what people don't like about us than we are to hear what we do well. This activity gives your group members a chance to exchange kind words with each other.

 ## How to Prepare

1. Gather the supplies listed in the "What You'll Need" box. Decorate the back of the mirror with a smiling face, hair, ears, eyelashes or whatever else you think of.
2. Read the "How to Lead" section to be sure you understand the activity.

 ## How to Lead

1. Begin the affirmation right after the Bible study. Introduce the activity by saying: One way we can help other people see the good in themselves is by pointing it out to them. In this activity, we'll each give our neighbor a mirror so they can see in themselves the positive things we see in them. I'll begin.
2. Hold the mirror out in front of you and say something positive that you want to give to the person sitting on your right. For example, you could say: I give Gloria a mirror so she can see how much her love for Christ shows in all she does. Or: I give Jim a mirror because he's so organized. I really admire him for that.
3. Go around the circle giving each group member a chance to share.

Togetherness

What You'll Need

- ☐ Wooden blocks (from the community-builder)

Time Needed:

5 minutes

The closing brings you back to the frustrating block towers you built in the community-builder. But there's a difference this time. This activity shows how, with cooperation and teamwork, you can accomplish tasks that are otherwise frustrating and difficult.

How to Prepare

1. Gather the blocks from the community-builder. Check with the leader to coordinate the activities.

2. Read the "How to Lead" section to be sure you understand the activity.

How to Lead

1. After the affirmation, have the group form a circle on the floor where you did the community-builder at the beginning of the meeting. Put the blocks in the center of the circle.

2. If possible, have group members each pick the same block they used in the community-builder. But if they can't remember which block they had, they can pick any block. Don't rush people; give them the time they need.

3. Explain that you're going to build a block tower again. But this time the rules are different. Tell them these guidelines:

● Group members will cooperate and help each other. For example, if you see someone with a bigger block than yours, let that person go ahead of you so the tower will be stronger.

● We'll plan a strategy before we build. Group members with big blocks will go first, medium-size blocks next, and then the smaller blocks will go on last. All group members will work to make it easy for others to add to the tower.

● Finally, we won't rush. But we'll still finish in five minutes.

4. Begin building the tower together. Have fun, and keep group members from getting upset if something goes wrong. If the tower falls, start again, and repeat the rules and goals so everyone understands them.

5. When the tower is done, lead a cheer: Yea, we did it!

6. Close the meeting with a song that fits the meeting. A good choice would be "The Building Block" by Noel Paul Stookey (in *Songs*, from Songs and Creations, Inc.). Then close with prayer, asking God to help you reach out to people in need and learn to cope with the stresses of everyday life.

7. After the meeting, serve refreshments.

Building Bridges Through Family Communication

MEETING 10

In our busy lives, we rarely stop to think about how we communicate in our families. So it's easy to avoid problems, pretending they don't exist. It's also easy to yell and scream at each other without even knowing what we're fighting about. This meeting for parents and teenagers together encourages families to improve communication.

Objectives

Parents and teenagers will:
- learn to look at problems from the other person's point of view;
- learn to solve problems by evaluating and compromising;
- listen to and consider each other's feelings; and
- express positive feelings toward each other.

Biblical Foundation

The parables of the lost sheep, the lost coin and the prodigal son (Luke 15:1-32) remind us that we need to share feelings, recognize each family member's needs and stress love in our families.

Adult Leader's Responsibilities

1. Meet with the meeting coordinator at least three weeks in advance. Help the coordinator find people to lead each aspect of the meeting. Have the coordinator arrange a meeting with the meeting leaders to coordinate efforts two weeks before the meeting.

2. Check with the publicity and invitation leaders to be sure they've completed their responsibilities.

3. Work with each leader to be sure he or she has all the supplies necessary for the meeting.

4. Call all leaders to make sure they get their materials ready before the meeting. Go over the checklists with each leader.

5. Remind leaders to ask other group members for help.

Meeting Coordinator's Responsibilities

1. Photocopy the instructions of each part of the meeting to give to the leaders.

2. At least three weeks before the meeting, find group members to be in charge of every aspect of the meeting. (If you wish, you may lead one of the sections yourself.) Give leaders each a photocopy of the element they're leading. Encourage leaders to find helpers if they need them.

3. Schedule a planning session two weeks before the event with all leaders to go through the meeting to be sure everyone understands it.

4. Tell the person responsible for invitations to ask other group members to help make invitations to send to parents. Be sure the invitation includes the meeting time, the place, the date and a brief description of the meeting. Make the invitation creative and fun (see Sample 10-1, "Invitation").

5. Encourage the publicity person to publicize the meeting in every way possible beginning *at least* two weeks in advance. Include write-ups in your church newsletter, and the Sunday bulletin. Hang colorful posters around the church. Announce the meeting in church at least two weeks in advance.

6. Find someone to coordinate refreshments for the evening. If you want, you can have a potluck dinner in conjunction with the meeting. (Ask some parents to help arrange the dinner.) Or serve pineapple upside-down cake and punch after the "Trading Places" activity.

7. Draft some friends to clean up after the meeting. Ask them ahead of time so they don't disappear right after the closing.

8. The day before the meeting, call all the leaders to make sure that they're ready for the meeting.

Meeting Outline				
Coordinator: _____				
Activity	**Estimated Time**	**Who's Responsible**	**Telephone**	**Confirmed**
Publicity				
Invitations				
Community-Builder: My Family	15 minutes			
Discussion-Starter: Trading Places	30 minutes			
Learning Time: Family Sharing	15 minutes			
Bible Study: Feeling Lost	10 minutes			
Affirmation: The Family Tree	10 minutes			
Closing: I'm a Fantastic Person	10 minutes			
Refreshments				

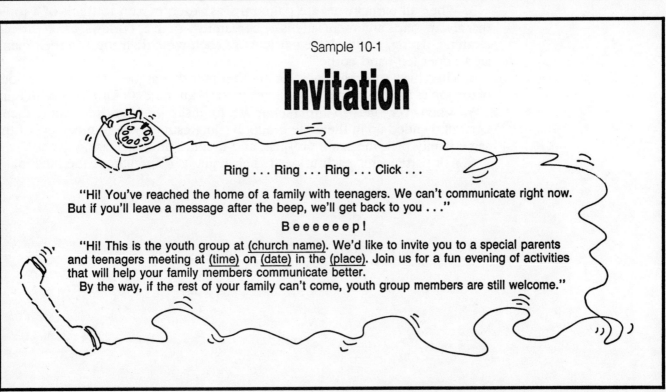

Sample 10-1

Invitation

Ring . . . Ring . . . Ring . . . Click . . .

"Hi! You've reached the home of a family with teenagers. We can't communicate right now. But if you'll leave a message after the beep, we'll get back to you . . ."

B e e e e e e p!

"Hi! This is the youth group at (church name). We'd like to invite you to a special parents and teenagers meeting at (time) on (date) in the (place). Join us for a fun evening of activities that will help your family members communicate better.

By the way, if the rest of your family can't come, youth group members are still welcome."

My Family

What You'll Need

☐ 3×5 cards
☐ Markers
☐ Masking tape

Time Needed:

15 minutes

Every family agrees on some things but disagrees on others. This community-builder helps parents and teenagers think about things they like to do together and what they always disagree about. In the process, everyone gets to know everyone else a little better.

How to Prepare

1. Gather the supplies listed in the "What You'll Need" box, and have them ready when everyone arrives.

2. Read the "How to Lead" section to be sure you understand the activity. If you want, practice leading the activity with a few friends.

How to Lead

1. As group members and parents arrive, give each a 3×5 card, a marker and a piece of masking tape for a name tag. Have them each write their name in their card's upper right-hand corner. Ask everyone to draw in the middle of the card a picture of his or her family doing something together that makes them all happy. For example, a picture may show family members camping in the mountains, going to a ball game or watching television together. Allow about five minutes. Then have people each tape on their name tag.

2. To get people into pairs, say: Now, mingle around the room until you find someone from another family who enjoys an activity similar to the one you drew on your name tag. These don't have to be exact matches. For example, any two things about sports can match, and any two outdoor activities—gardening, hiking, or swimming—can match.

Allow about five minutes for everyone to find a partner. If there's an extra person, have one group include three people.

3. When all participants are paired up, ask each person to think of a topic that always starts arguments in his or her family—such as curfews, using the car, cleaning, dating, grades. Have participants each write their topic in their name tag's upper left-hand corner.

4. Then have each pair look for another pair that argues about one or both of the topics on their name tags. Allow about five minutes to form groups of four.

5. When everyone's in a foursome, ask for a show of hands of family members who ended up in the same group. It's interesting to see if members of the same family pick the same problem and if some problems are universal.

6. Ask participants each to wear their name tag throughout the meeting.

Trading Places

What You'll Need

☐ Props to help everyone get into the mood for reversing roles—these could include bathrobes, curlers, old shirts, jackets, hats, chairs and tables (for a living room or kitchen setting), newspapers (to read or clip coupons), radios, posters of your favorite stars and so forth

☐ "Trading Places" handout (Handout 10-2)—one per family

Time Needed:

30 minutes

Often we're so wound up in our own ideas and feelings that we don't think about how other people feel. This role-reversal game helps people see a situation from another person's point of view—parents will see the teenagers' viewpoint and teenagers will see the parents' viewpoint. In this game, parents and teenagers exchange places—teenagers become parents, and parents become teenagers.

How to Prepare

1. Gather the supplies listed in the "What You'll Need" box. Put a box of props in each room you'll be using.

2. Read the "How to Lead" section to be sure you understand the activity.

3. Recruit some assistants to help organize and lead the game by taking charge of one room during the activity. Give them instructions and questions to use while leading.

4. Get permission to use enough rooms in the church building so that you'll have no more than 20 people in each room. For example, if you expect 25 teenagers and 35 parents, you'll need three rooms. Make sure the rooms are available and unlocked during your meeting time.

How to Lead

1. When the community-builder is finished, have participants get together with their own families. Have smaller families "adopt" any teenagers whose parents didn't attend.

2. When all families are together, assign each family to a designated room so they're spread evenly (no more than four or five families per room).

3. Then say: Tonight the tables turn. From now on, all parents are teenagers, and all teenagers are parents. Everyone's switching roles. Go to your designated room where you'll prepare a skit using reversed roles. You'll pick a situation from a handout and role play how to solve the problem as a "role-reversed" family.

4. When families are in their rooms, have your assistants distribute the "Trading Places" handout (Handout 10-2) to each family. Have assistants ask each family to enact a situation from the handout. Families in each room can compare notes with other families so that they don't all do the same skit.

5. Have assistants give families about five minutes to prepare skits. They can encourage families each to rummage through the prop box in their room to find appropriate props for their skit.

6. When everyone is ready, the assistants should ask each family to present its skit to the other families in the room. After each skit, the assistants ask the players to tell what they learned from the role reversal. Questions to ask include:

● How does it feel to reverse roles with other family members?

● What did you learn about being teenagers or parents?

● How might this exercise change the way you interact with other family members?

7. When families complete all the skits, have them go back to the main meeting room.

Trading Places

In this exercise, family members exchange roles in a conflict situation. Parents become teenagers, and teenagers become parents. This fun exercise helps you better understand what it's like to be a teenager or a parent today.

Pick one of the following eight conflicts to role play. To avoid duplication, tell other groups in your room what you're doing. Then develop a three-minute skit to show your "reversed" family's response to the situation. You may use the props in the box. Your skit should include:

(1) the events leading up to the problem;
(2) the point of conflict; and
(3) how the whole family works out the problem.

Some situations only mention two family members. But any conflict really involves the whole family. So you can add characters if you like. You may also change the characters' names to fit your family. Be creative and have fun.

Conflicts

1. Caroline is 15; her friend Jan is only 14. Jan's boyfriend, Dan, just turned 16 and can drive his family's car. Jan and Dan have asked Caroline and Bob, Dan's 15-year-old friend, to go to the movies with them Friday night. Until now, Caroline has gone with guys only to school and church functions. This would be her first date. So she has to ask her mom if she can go. How should she ask her? What should she say? Why?

2. Mark doesn't like making his bed. His mother complains when he doesn't make the bed, so he always tries to sneak out of the house before she notices that his bed isn't made. Mark's dad doesn't think making the bed is important, so Mark always seeks his dad's support when the topic comes up. Is it fair for Mark to get his dad to side with him against his mother? Should Mark's mother insist that Mark make his bed every morning? What could the family do to resolve the conflict?

3. Vicki doesn't like doing homework and doesn't see any value in it. Her last report card had three B's, one A and one C. Vicki's dad was angry and said she has to study at least two hours every night. Vicki thinks this rule is unfair. Vicki's mom also wants her to help with the supper dishes. Vicki says she won't have time to help if she has to study for two hours. Do you think the homework regulations are fair or unfair? What should the family do to resolve all the conflicts?

4. Jose, a freshman, is a middle child. His sister, Maria, is a senior. His brother, Juan, is in fifth grade. Maria always goes to school activities on Friday nights. Most functions end by 10, but Maria doesn't have to be home until 11:30. However, Jose has to be home by 10:30. Jose feels the 10:30 curfew is too early, especially since he can stay up until 12:30 on Friday night when he's home. On the other hand, Maria thinks changing Jose's curfew would be unfair, since she had to be home at 10:30 when she was Jose's age. Juan insists that his curfew be extended if Jose's is. How should Jose's parents respond? What would you do if you were Jose?

5. Linda's father won't let her go to Paul's party because he doesn't know Paul's parents. He's also worried that there won't be enough adults supervising the party. Lots of Linda's friends will be at the party, and she feels it's unfair that she can't go. How could Linda persuade her father to change his mind? How will her father react?

6. Every year the Morgans spend their Christmas vacation in Florida. They leave the week before Christmas, so they don't decorate their house or participate in many Christmas activities. Mark's youth group presents a Christmas play, goes caroling and makes decorations for shut-ins. But Mark can't participate because of the family trip. Mark's parents are already talking about next year's plans. Mark doesn't want to go. What can he do? How can Mark explain his feelings to his parents? How should they respond?

7. Mrs. Kilgore is a church board member, and Mr. Kilgore teaches Sunday school. Annette doesn't like church, but her parents force her to go. The Kilgores just learned that Annette hasn't been in Sunday school for almost a month. Instead, she and some friends have met near a rarely used staircase in the church basement during Sunday school to talk and play cards. How should Annette's parents respond? What should Annette say if confronted about skipping Sunday school?

8. Jim is an only child. Jim's mom is having the house repainted. She asked Jim what color he wants in his room, and Jim said orange. His mom said no. What should Jim do? What should Jim's mom do?

Family Sharing

What You'll Need

☐ Paper and markers
☐ Tables and chairs

Time Needed:

15 minutes

Talking about our feelings and problems and saying kind words to our families aren't always easy. And it's also hard to break bad habits of yelling and arguing. This activity gives a positive way to deal with differences by discussing a problem instead of fighting about it.

How to Prepare

1. Gather the supplies listed in the "What You'll Need" box.
2. Read the "How to Lead" section to be sure you understand the activity.

How to Lead

1. After the discussion-starter skits are finished, ask participants to get into their regular or "adopted" families again. They won't be reversing roles anymore.

2. Give each family paper and markers. Then say: One person in each family needs to draw a bridge on the family's paper. It can be a fancy arch bridge, a covered bridge or just a plain, straight bridge like you see across the highway.

3. When the bridges are drawn, ask families each to designate a scribe to write under their bridge a problem their family frequently argues or disagrees about. To help people think of something, remind them that they can use the topics on their name tags.

4. Next, have each family list, at the right end of their bridge, the positive issues related to the problem, and on the left end, the negative issues. If parents and teenagers always argue about curfews, they might say that a positive side is that parents care about their teenager and teenagers want to show they can be responsible for their actions. Allow about five minutes.

5. Then announce that it's time to begin family sharing time. Ask families each to look at the problem they outlined and think of a compromise to write across the top of their bridge. The compromise must be something everyone agrees with, even if no one gets everything exactly his or her way. Give families plenty of time to work through their solutions.

BIBLE STUDY: Feeling Lost

What You'll Need

☐ Bibles
☐ Newsprint
☐ Marker
☐ Chairs

Time Needed:

10 minutes

Have you ever felt that no one cared about you? This Bible study focuses on two brothers who both felt left out of their families. It focuses on how they and their families responded to those feelings.

How to Prepare

1. Gather the supplies listed in the "What You'll Need" box.

2. Write the following references on newsprint: Luke 15:1-7, 8-10 and 11-32.

3. Write the following questions on a separate sheet of newsprint:

● How did the younger brother feel about his older brother?

● Do we worry as much about hurting someone's feelings as we do about losing something expensive? Explain.

● Do we spend as much time helping a friend who is hurting as the woman spent looking for the coin? Why or why not?

4. Read the "How to Lead" section to be sure you understand the activity. Practice telling the story out loud several times. It doesn't have to be word for word. If you feel unsure of yourself, just read the story. But don't be afraid to tell the story from memory, giving it your own special touch.

How to Lead

1. When the family sharing time is over, gather everyone in a circle of chairs. Tell the "Jacobs Family Story" (Sample 10-3).

2. After the story, have participants form teams of six to eight, with both adults and young people in each team. They don't have to stay with their families. Then send each team to a separate area of the room to form a small circle.

3. When the teams are each together in their circle, say: Each team needs to decide what it would do if it were in the Jacobs family's situation.

4. As they discuss the story, give each team a Bible. Post both the newsprint sheet with questions and the sheet with Bible references so everyone can see them. Tell teams to read the passages and then answer the posted questions.

5. Next, have each team look for similarities between Michael feeling lost and the parables Jesus told. Allow about five minutes for the discussion.

6. When the time has elapsed, ask each team to report on its insights.

Sample 10-3

Jacobs Family Story

Gary, Michael and Jane live with their mom and dad in a nice neighborhood. Gary's the oldest, and Jane's the youngest—which leaves Michael in the middle between a popular big brother and an adorable little sister.

Michael feels lost between the two. Of course, Michael tries to keep up with Gary, but he always seems to fall short. Michael's parents try to emphasize what Michael does well, but it never seems to be quite enough when compared to Gary's ribbons, trophies and newspaper articles. Michael feels like a nobody. So he has crept further and further into his shell. He barely passes in school; he has no friends left because he doesn't bother to spend time with them; and he's even stopped working on his favorite hobby: building models.

You see, Michael has this talent for building models. He can build models of anything from anything. Once he made a Western fort out of toothpicks—complete with a swinging gate, wagons, and houses with windows, doors and lift-off roofs to show the furniture inside. Michael's parents are particularly proud of his creativity, and they point it out every chance they get. And each model has a special place in the house.

But Michael doesn't feel that model-building is as important as what Gary does. Michael feels like his models are just "kid's stuff." His parents are concerned about him. They don't know what to do.

(Long pause and then ask the question.) If you were the Jacobs family, what would you do?

AFFIRMATION: The Family Tree

What You'll Need

☐ Paper and markers
☐ Tables and chairs
☐ Newsprint

Time Needed:

10 minutes

Sometimes when we think about our family members, we can think only of arguments, personality differences or something parents won't let us do. But we should also think of what's special about each person in our family. This exercise helps family members build up each other through positive affirmation.

How to Prepare

1. Gather the supplies listed in the "What You'll Need" box.
2. Set up tables for everyone to work around.
3. Draw a "family tree" on newsprint. Make it simple—a circle with a trunk is fine and gives plenty of space to write.
4. Read the "How to Lead" section to be sure you understand the activity.

How to Lead

1. After the Bible study, ask people to gather around tables with their families.
2. Give everyone a piece of paper and a marker.
3. Then give these instructions while showing the tree you drew on newsprint: On your paper, draw a simple tree like this one. Leave plenty of room in the middle to write your family members' names. Then write on your tree the name of each family member. Next to each name, write what you admire most about that person. Allow about five minutes.
4. When everyone is finished, ask participants to show their family trees to the whole group and to describe their family members' outstanding traits.

CLOSING: I'm a Fantastic Person

What You'll Need

- ☐ Pastel construction paper for "I'm a Fantastic Person" badges (one for each participant)
- ☐ Markers
- ☐ Tape
- ☐ Chairs

Time Needed:

10 minutes

To close, send everyone home feeling good about the evening and the new friends they made. Give everyone the opportunity to say something positive to people they met this evening, using the "I'm a Fantastic Person" badges.

How to Prepare

1. Gather the supplies listed in the "What You'll Need" box.

2. Read the "How to Lead" section to be sure you understand the activity.

3. Prepare the "I'm a Fantastic Person" badges. Recruit friends to help you. Cut large circles, balloons or stars out of pastel construction paper, and write on each badge with different colored markers: "(a blank space for the person's name) is a fantastic person because . . ." Leave space on the badge so people can write why they think the person is fantastic. (See Sample 10-4, "Fantastic Badge.")

4. Find and prepare to lead a closing song (such as "Everything Is Beautiful" (in *Songs*, from Songs and Creations, Inc.) If possible, enlist a pianist or guitar player to accompany the singing. Otherwise, just make a joyful noise!

How to Lead

1. When the family tree affirmation is complete, get everyone together in a circle of chairs. Families don't need to stay together.

2. Give each person a badge and a colored marker. Then say: Everyone in this room is a fantastic person. On the badge you have, write one or two words that describe why the person sitting on your right is a fantastic person. For example, you could write: Tom is a fantastic person because he always has a smile.

3. When everyone is finished, ask participants each to tape the badge on their neighbor while reading what they wrote.

4. Lead the group in a song that affirms each person's gifts, such as "Jesus Made You to Be Beautiful" (in *Songs*, from Songs and Creations, Inc.).

5. Lead the group in your traditional closing or lead a prayer. Ask God to help your group appreciate the gifts he has given each person in the family of God. Send people home wearing the badges.

Sample 10-4

Fantastic Badge

ROSEANNE is a fantastic person because . . .